Talk About Literature

Talk About Literature

David F. Clarke

Edward Arnold
A division of Hodder & Stoughton
LONDON   MELBOURNE   AUCKLAND

© 1989 David F. Clarke

First published in Great Britain 1989

British Library Cataloguing in Publication Data

Talk about literature.
 1. English language. Readers — For non-English speaking students
 I. Clarke, David F
 428.6′4

ISBN 0-340-50440-4

All rights reserved. No part of this publication may be reproduced or transmitted in any form or by any means, electronically or mechanically, including photocopying, recording or any information storage or retrieval system, without either prior permission in writing from the publisher or a licence permitting restricted copying. In the United Kingdom such licences are issued by the Copyright Licensing Agency: 33-34 Alfred Place, London WC1E 7DP.

Typeset in Univers
by ATek Art Ltd
Printed and bound in Great Britain
for Edward Arnold, the educational, academic and medical publishing division of Hodder and Stoughton Limited, 41 Bedford Square, London WC1B 3DQ by The Bath Press, Avon

Acknowledgements

The publisher would like to thank the following for their permission to use copyright material:

Cadbury for 'Snow' by Juliet George from the *Cadbury's Fifth Book of Children's Poetry*; Jonathan Cape Ltd for the extract from 'The Big Two-Hearted River' by Ernest Hemingway from *In Our Time*; Chatto & Windus for the extract from *Cider with Rosie* by Laurie Lee; Curtis Brown and Michael Joseph for the extract from *A Kestrel for a Knave* by Barry Hines © Barry Hines 1968 reprinted by permission of Curtis Brown Ltd and Michael Joseph Ltd; Judy Daish Associates Ltd for the extract from *Stand Up Nigel Barton* by Dennis Potter; Faber & Faber Ltd for 'Toads Revisited' by Philip Larkin from *The Whitsun Weddings*; Harmony Music Ltd for 'What did you learn in school today' by Tom Paxton © Harmony Music Ltd, 1a Farm Place, London W8 7SX, International Copyright Secured. All Rights Reserved. Used by permission; A M Heath, the estate of the late Sonia Brownell-Orwell and Secker and Warburg Ltd for the extract from *Down and Out in Paris and London* by George Orwell; Methuen London for the extract from *Room at the Top* by John Braine; James Matthews for the extract from *The Park*; Tessa Sayle for the extract from *Saturday Night and Sunday Morning* by Alan Sillitoe reprinted by permission of Tessa Sayle Agency; Unwin Hyman for 'Lazy Man's Song' from *Chinese Poems* translated by Arthur Waley; Warner Chappell Music Ltd for 'Material Girl' author and composers: Peter H Brown and Robert S Rans © 1985 Minong Pub Co, reproduced by permission of Warner Chappell Music Ltd and 'Puff the Magic Dragon' author and composers: Peter Yarrow and Leonard Lipton © 1962 Pepamar Music Corp, reproduced by permission of Warner Chappell Music Ltd.

Photographs: Barnaby's Picture Library pp. 1, 13, 14, 26, 45, 85, 98 and 103; Janine Wiedel p. 23; Anthony MacAvoy p. 26; Steve Richards p. 65; BBC Enterprises p. 70; Ronald Watts p. 103.

Artwork: Taurus Graphics.

Every effort has been made to trace copyright holders of material reproduced in this book. Any rights not acknowledged here will be acknowledged in subsequent printings if notice is given to the publisher.

Contents

General Introduction

The Golden Gates of Childhood   1

The Echoing Green, William Blake; *David Copperfield*, Charles Dickens; *Plumbers*, Susan Miles; *Sons and Lovers*, D H Lawrence; *The Swing*, R L Stevenson; *The Park*, James Matthews; *Stand Up Nigel Barton*, Dennis Potter; *Puff the Magic Dragon*, Peter Yarrow and Paul Lipton.

The Happiest Days of Your Life   23

Hard Times, Charles Dickens; *The Schoolboy*, William Blake; *What did you learn in school today?* Tom Paxton; *A Kestrel for a Knave*, Barry Hines; *Cider with Rosie*, Laurie Lee; *The Essay*, Ellen Jackson.

All Work and No Play   45

Lazy Man's Song, Po Chu-i; *Martin Eden*, Jack London; *Saturday Night and Sunday Morning*, Alan Sillitoe; *What is he?* D H Lawrence; *Walden*, Henry David Thoreau; *Toads Revisited*, Philip Larkin; *Down and Out in Paris and London*, George Orwell.

The Root of all Evil   65

Silas Marner, George Eliot; *The Moon Cannot Be Stolen*, Buddhist Story; *The Green Leaves*, Grace Ogot; *Material Girl*, Madonna; *Room at the Top*, John Braine.

The World of Nature   85

I Wandered Lonely as a Cloud, William Wordsworth; *Diary Extract*, Dorothy Wordsworth; Alfred Lord Tennyson; *Haiku*, Basho; *Haiku*, Chiyo; *Haikus*, Basho; *Jude the Obscure*, Thomas Hardy; *Big Two Hearted River*, Ernest Hemingway; *London Snow*, Robert Bridges; *Snow*, Juliet George; *Haiku*, Boncho; *Haikus*, Basho; *The Village Priest*, James Ngugi; *An African Thunderstorm*, David Rubadiri.

Tapescripts   109

Key   111

General Introduction

> I would put a child into a library (where no unfit books are) and let him read at his choice. A child should not be discouraged from reading any thing that he takes a liking to, from a notion that it is above his reach. If that be the case, the child will soon find it out and desist; if not, he of course gains instruction; which is so much the more likely to come, from the inclination with which he takes up the study.
>
> Samuel Johnson

> Unfortunately we English teachers are easily hung up on this matter of understanding. Why should children understand everything they read? Why should anyone? *Does* anyone? I don't, and never did. I was always reading books that teachers said were 'too hard' for me, books full of words I didn't know. That's how I got to be a good teacher.
>
> *The Underachieving School*, John Holt

Contents and purpose of the book

Talk About Literature is intended for students of English as a second or foreign language at the intermediate or upper intermediate level. This material can be used as a core course where reading and speaking are of central interest but it can also be integrated within a general English course when a variety of textual input is required.

The book is a collection of literary texts, poetry, prose and drama, arranged in five theme areas relating to the following subjects:

1 childhood
2 school and education
3 work and employment
4 money
5 the natural world.

Literary texts have been chosen in order to provide an extra dimension in a language course which perhaps contains little to engage the learner at an emotional level. The texts offer varying approaches to the different themes, which have been selected because of their potential relevance to the experience of the learners. After working with one or two of the texts provided, most learners should be able to say something about their experience of childhood or their attitude to work and money.

There are six or more texts within each of the theme areas, which are divided for convenience of use into several Parts. Each of the texts is accompanied by a number of tasks or activities which lead learners to investigate different aspects of what they are reading. Some of the prose passages are a good deal longer than a single paragraph, the intention being to provide a substantial amount of reading material and not to focus on short texts in excessive detail. The theme-based structure was thus selected in order to allow time and space for the development of an extended and meaningful context for reading and discussion.

Unedited authentic texts, as used in *Talk About Literature*, will inevitably produce some linguistic difficulties. However, since the book's intention is to provide fairly extensive reading, learners are advised to ignore those details which are difficult and are not explained because they are not relevant to the completion of the suggested tasks. The activities or tasks accompanying the texts can be undertaken without complete understanding of every word in the texts. General appreciation of the texts is also perfectly possible without having to solve every lexical or syntactic problem.

Rather than simplifying texts, therefore, the procedure has been to select a series of tasks or activities which will draw learners' attention to the most important aspects of each text through a process of discovery. The use of tasks has been chosen in order to avoid asking blunt and often unanswerable questions about the texts. The texts are thus not treated as excuses for asking numerous "comprehension questions" but rather opportunities are provided to explore different aspects of what the text contains. When questions *are* asked about the text, it is hoped that the preceding tasks will have put the learners in a reasonable position to respond to them.

Following the five theme areas, a Key is provided to facilitate self-study and self-correction, either in or outside the classroom. Suggested responses to the tasks are provided in most cases. Those tasks which have no Key comment have self-explanatory responses or involve uncontrolled discussion and exchange of opinion.

Use of the book and methodology

A flexible approach

As indicated, *Talk About Literature* has been designed so that it can be used according to different requirements, either in a classroom situation or for self-study. A large variety of texts and tasks have been included in the book. While a chronological approach to the material could be taken, it is intended that the book can also be used in a more flexible way. Within the theme areas it is not *necessary* to read all the texts and undertake all the tasks. Depending on the time available, teachers are invited to make a selection based on the interests of the learners. While most of the texts do form specific links with those nearby, and indeed with those in other sections, there is no reason why they cannot be treated separately. Theme areas have been divided into Parts to create smaller blocks of work, and each Part contains texts with particularly close links with each other. It will probably be useful to keep the Parts intact but otherwise there is no reason why certain texts, tasks or whole Parts should not simply be omitted in the interests of economy. It is hoped, however, that learners' curiosity might lead them to explore other texts within a particular theme area.

Just as the texts can be selected as required, it is likewise not necessary that all tasks should be attempted. Selection can be left to the discretion of the teacher or perhaps to the learners themselves on some occasions. Alternatively, a teacher may add to the list of tasks if it seems appropriate by taking examples of task types from other texts and adapting them.

Working Methods

The rubric to each of the tasks provides a format which may be followed but may, again, be changed according to different classroom circumstances. There are three basic formats or rubrics:

1. It is sometimes suggested that learners work in pairs to attempt the task in order to generate more ideas.
2. It is frequently suggested that learners work in two sets. This simply involves the teacher dividing the class into two sections, A and B. Whenever the "Work in two sets" instruction occurs, the two sections of the class can attempt different tasks. Within the large sets, learners are asked to work in pairs, but this can be altered to "work alone" if a teacher sees this as a preferable mode.

    The procedure of working in two sets is partly one of economy, so that more exploration of the text can take place in less time. More importantly, however, the process allows certain learners to become "expert" on certain aspects of the text, thus allowing genuine communication with the other set about what they have discovered. Each set can either report its findings to the other set (who can be asked to note down what they are told about) or they can ask members of the other set questions about what they have discovered. In this way, learners are not always working in "lock-step", thus providing a greater degree of variety.
3. Sometimes it is indicated that the whole class should attempt a particular task as individuals.

It is of course possible to adapt or dispense with the suggestions offered in the rubrics. It might be seen as desirable, for example, for pairs to work through the tasks of *both* sets A and B, or indeed for an individual learner

General Introduction xi

to go through them in a self-study situation. Again, it can be left to the teacher to decide which mode is preferrable. The A and B tasks have been provided to allow a differentiated approach if this seems suitable.

Handling of specific tasks

In many of the tasks learners are asked to make lists in pairs. These lists might be of words and phrases which learners find in a text or they might be summaries of their personal opinions and ideas. The tasks then often request the learners to "report their ideas to the class". At this report stage, teachers might find it useful to collate on the board the suggestions made in order to provide a summary of what has been done. This is particularly useful in the case of prediction activities when the suggested predictions will be compared with what actually occurs in the text.

A number of vocabulary tasks involve learners being asked to check that they know the meaning of a list of words prior to reading the text from which the words come. This process can involve the learners discussing the meanings in pairs, using a dictionary (as is usually suggested) or asking the teacher as she walks around the classroom. Indeed, all three sources of information can be employed together or singly at the teacher's discretion. There should then be a follow-up stage, using either L1 or L2 to check that the learners have managed to discover the meaning of the words in the list. If the task has been done in two sets, then this monitoring procedure is operated by members of one set asking members of the others about the meaning of unknown words.

A number of tasks involve the use of taped material and of course the number of playings of each text must be left to the discretion of the teacher. The teacher can also decide whether the tape should be played while the learners are reading or whether it should be used as a pure listening activity. In cases where songs are used, the teacher can attempt to obtain a recording of the original songs to use in the class.

Theme 1 The Golden Gates of Childhood

Part 1

Text A Introductory Texts

a. Let the little children come to me; do not try to prevent them; for the kingdom of God belongs to such as these.

The Bible

The Golden Gates of Childhood

b. I'd give all the wealth that years have piled,
   The slow result of life's decay,
   To be once more a little child
   For one bright summer's day

   Lewis Carroll

c. Let dogs delight to bark and bite,
   For God hath made them so:
   Let bears and lions growl and fight,
   For 'tis their nature too.

   But, children, you should never let
   Such angry passions rise;
   Your little hands were never made
   To tear each other's eyes.

   Isaac Watts

d. Any man who hates dogs and children can't be all bad.

   W.C. Fields

e. They had gone forth together into their new life of sorrow, and they would never more see the sunshine undimmed by remembered cares. They had entered the thorny wilderness, and the golden gates of their childhood had forever closed behind them.

   Mill on the Floss, George Eliot

f. Children should be seen and not heard

   Victorian advice

g. PETER: Would you send me to school?
   MRS DARLING: Yes.
   PETER: And then to the office?
   MRS DARLING: I suppose.
   PETER: Should I soon be a man?
   MRS DARLING: Very soon.
   PETER: I don't want to go to school and learn solemn things. No one is going to catch me, lady, and make me a man. I want always to be a little boy and to have fun.

   Peter Pan, J.M. Barrie

Glossary
cares: worries
thorny wilderness: dangerous wild place
solemn: serious

3 Talk About Literature

1.1 Discussion

Work in two sets, A and B. Within the sets, work in pairs. Look at the short texts above.

Set A should find out:
- which text matches the picture
- which texts say that childhood is a wonderful period of life

Set B should find out:
- which text is intended to be humorous
- which texts say something about the behaviour of children

Report to the class what you have discovered.

1.2 Looking at vocabulary

The first main text is a poem called "The Echoing Green" by William Blake. This poem presents another view of childhood.
Before you read the poem check in pairs that you know the meaning of the words below. Use a dictionary if necessary.

        echo   folk   youth   weary

1.3 Deciding on the mood of a text

Listen to the first verse of the poem and see if you can tell what mood the poem seems to have: happy or sad, positive or negative.

Text B The Echoing Green

> The sun does arise,
> And make happy the skies;
> The merry bells ring
> To welcome the Spring
> 5 The skylark and thrush,
> The birds of the bush,
> Sing louder around
> To the bell's cheerful sound,
> While our sports shall be seen
> 10 On the Echoing Green.

Now listen to the complete poem.

> Old John, with white hair,
> Does laugh away care,
> Sitting under the oak,
> Among the old folk.

15 They laugh at our play,
    And soon they all say:
    "Such, such were the joys
    When we all, girls and boys,
    In our youth time were seen
20 On the Echoing Green."

    Till the little ones, weary,
    No more can be merry;
    The sun does descend,
    And our sports have an end.
25 Round the laps of their mothers
    Many sisters and brothers,
    Like birds in their nest,
    Are ready for rest,
    And sport no more seen
30 On the darkening Green.

William Blake (1789)

Glossary

Green: open area of grass. The village green is the open area at the centre of many villages

9 *sports:* games

25 *lap:* when you are seated, your lap is between your waist and your knees. Children sit on their mothers' laps

1.4 Looking at language and meaning

Work in two sets, A and B. Within the sets, work in pairs. Find out the following things.

Set A

List all the **sounds** or **noises** you can find in the poem. Look for the two different speakers in the poem.

Set B

Look for the two main contrasts or opposite ideas in the poem. In the last verse the sun goes down and the green becomes dark. Try to think of any possible extra meaning for these ideas.

Report to the class what you have found.

"Echo" is also used by Blake with an **extra meaning**. The sounds of the children playing might echo on the green. But there is also the echo of the memory of childhood experienced by the old people.

5 Talk About Literature

Part 2

2.1 Making a class survey

How far can you remember back? How long ago is your earliest memory?

Count how the class votes on these questions:
  Is your earliest memory a person or a thing?
  Are smells an important part of your early memories?
  Are your early memories mostly pleasant or unpleasant?

Text C is taken from *David Copperfield* by Charles Dickens. Near the beginning of the book David tries to remember as far back into his childhood as he can. David's father is dead and Peggotty is a woman who helps his mother with cooking, cleaning and looking after David.

2.2 Deciding on the mood of a text

As you read, decide which of these words best describes the mood of Text C.

happiness   fear   sadness   anger   worry   humour

Text C

What else do I remember? Let me see?
There comes out of the cloud, our house – not new to me, but quite familiar, in its earliest remembrance. On the ground-floor is Peggotty's kitchen, opening into a back-yard; with a pigeon-house
5 on a pole, in the centre, without any pigeons in it; a great dog-kennel in a corner, without any dog; and a quantity of fowls that look terribly tall to me, walking about, in a menacing and ferocious manner. There is one cock who gets upon a post to crow, and seems to take particular notice of me as I look at him through the kitchen
10 window, who makes me shiver, he is so fierce. Of the geese outside the side-gate who come waddling after me with their long necks stretched out when I go that way, I dream at night: as a man environed by wild beasts might dream of lions.
Here is a long passage – what an enormous perspective I made of
15 it! – leading from Peggotty's kitchen to the front-door. A dark store-room opens out of it, and that is a place to be run past at night; for I don't know what may be among those tubs and jars and old tea-chests, when there is nobody in there with a dimly-burning light, letting a mouldy air come out at the door, in which there is the
20 smell of soap, pickles, pepper, candles, and coffee, all at one whiff. Then there are the two parlours: the parlour in which we sit of an evening, my mother and I and Peggotty – for Peggotty is quite our

companion, when her work is done and we are alone – and the best parlour where we sit on a Sunday; grandly, but not so comfortably.
25 There is something of a doleful air about that room to me, for Peggotty has told me – I don't know when, but apparently ages ago – about my father's funeral, and the company having their black cloaks put on. One Sunday night my mother reads to Peggotty and me in there, how Lazarus was raised up from the dead. And I am
30 so frightened that they are afterwards obliged to take me out of bed, and show me the quiet churchyard out of the bedroom-window, with the dead all lying in their graves at rest, below the solemn moon.

David Copperfield, Charles Dickens (1850)

Glossary
6 *fowls* : chickens
7 *menacing* : threatening, looking dangerous
8 *cock* : male chicken
10 *shiver* : shake with fear
14 *perspective* : distance
17 *tubs* : large round containers
19 *mouldy* : stale, not fresh
25 *doleful* : gloomy, sad
29 *Lazarus was raised up from the dead* : a reference to a story in *The Bible* where Jesus Christ causes a dead man called Lazarus to live again
30 *obliged to* : forced to

2.3 Guessing the meaning of words

In pairs, try to guess the meaning of the following words by looking at where they are found in the text.

pigeon   dog-kennel   ferocious   parlour

2.4 Finding out how mood is created

Work in two sets, A and B. Within the sets, work in pairs.

Set A

List all the things which frighten David.

Set B

List all the words connected with being frightened.

Ask members of the other set about what they have discovered.

Does Dickens successfully create the mood of childhood fear? Is there anything in the text which reminds you of your own childhood?

7   Talk About Literature

2.5   Looking at verb forms

Which verb form, present or past, would you use for telling a story?

Now work in two sets, A and B. Within the sets, work in pairs.

Set A

Count how many verbs are in the present form in the first 15 lines.

Set B

Count how many verbs are in the present form in the last 18 lines.

Are there any examples of the past form being used? Why do you think Dickens uses so many present forms?
Imagine that Dickens had used the past forms for all his verbs. Do you think the story would sound better?

2.6   Discussion

Work in pairs and list the things which frightened you as a child. Compare your ideas with the class.

Part 3

Peggotty in Text C was not David Copperfield's mother but she looked after him and was very kind to him. A woman who looked after the children in a family was sometimes called a "nurse", as in Text D.

The Golden Gates of Childhood 8

3.1 Looking at a picture and predicting

What are the happiest and most exciting times of the year for a child? Does the picture give you any idea about which of these might be mentioned in Text D? What else do you think this text might be about? Make a list on the blackboard.

3.2 Looking at vocabulary

Before you read Text D, look at some of the words you will find in it. Work in two sets, A and B. Within the sets, work in pairs. Match the words with the explanations below. Use a dictionary if necessary.

Set A

plumber, icicle, selfish

Set B

frost, wire netting, choke (verb)

- metal material used for making fences you can see through
- not being concerned about the needs of others
- a person who mends pipes and water systems
- a long thin pointed piece of ice
- a white substance which appears on very cold days
- having difficulty with swallowing, which causes coughing

Ask members of the other set if you do not know the meaning of any of their words.

3.3 Listening and comparing

Listen to the poem and look again at the picture. Note down which things in the picture are mentioned in the poem.

Text D Plumbers

   I knew that in winter it would snow,
   For my brother had told me.
   I knew that snow was white
   And soft
 5 And altogether wonderful;
   But how white and soft and wonderful
   I did not know,
   Being too young to remember
   Winter.
10 One day snow fell;
   And the garden
   Was a new garden;

          The trees were new trees.
          There were icicles.
    15   I marvelled that my brother
          Had forgotten to tell me
          That there would be icicles.
          How could a child see icicles
          And not remember?
    20   Or frost on wire-netting,
          And not tell?
          I was happier than on my birthday;
          I was happier than on Christmas morning.
          "Selfish little pig,"
    25   Said Nurse.
          "You don't think of the poor plumbers;
          Nor you don't think of their poor children.
          No breakfast for them, poor lambs!
          No nice porridge,
    30   No bacon fat;
          Not when the poor plumbers can't work
          On account of the frost.
          No fun in the snow,
          Not for them.
    35   They wouldn't have the heart.
          No more would you have the heart,
          Not without you were a selfish little pig."
          And my bacon fat choked me,
          Because of the bitter knowledge
    40   That one couldn't love icicles
          Nor frost on wire-netting,
          Because of people called plumbers:
          – Not without one was a selfish
          Little pig.

Susan Miles (1917)

Glossary

35   *They wouldn't have the heart* : they wouldn't feel like enjoying themselves
36   *No more would you . . . little pig* : you wouldn't enjoy yourself either,
          unless you were a selfish little pig

3.4   Finding out how mood is created

First work in pairs and find a good place to break the poem into two parts. Then work in two sets A and B. Within the sets, work in pairs. Look at **positive** and **negative** words in the poem. "Fun" (33) on its own would be an example of a positive word but it is made into a negative idea by adding "no" before it.

The Golden Gates of Childhood 10

Set A	Set B
List the positive and negative words or ideas in the first half.	List the positive and negative words or ideas in the second half.

Report to the class what you have found.
What sort of person is the nurse? Is she positive or negative, kind or unkind?

3.5 Comparing rhyme schemes

Sometimes poets make words at the end of lines rhyme with other words. Look back to the short text by Isaac Watts at the beginning of this section. The first line rhymes with the third lines ("bite" and "fight") but the second line does not rhyme with the fourth ("so" and "too"). This rhyme scheme is given the letter code ABAC. In the second verse the rhyme scheme changes to ABCB, where the second and fourth lines rhyme.
Work in two sets, A and B. Within the sets, work in pairs. Set A should look at the rhyme scheme of Text B and Set B should look at the rhyme scheme of Text D. Write down the letter code.
Report what you have found to the other set and give examples of words that rhyme. Compare the rhyme schemes of Text D with Text C.

Which of these rhyme schemes do you prefer?

3.6 Looking at vocabulary

As an introduction to Text E, find out the meaning of some of the words from this text.
Work in two sets, A and B. Within the sets, work in pairs. Use a dictionary if necessary.

Set A	Set B
sweep (verb)	drumming
snarl (verb)	shriek
fierce	drown
conflict (noun)	suspense
anxiety	horror

Ask members of the other set about any of their words you do not know. Now, in pairs, note down any ideas the words in your list are often linked with. For example, "sweep" is often linked with "brush" and "drumming" is often linked with music and bands.

"Plumbers" (Text D) is about a child's confusion when faced with an adult view of the world. In Text E, D.H. Lawrence also writes of the confusion and difficulties he had when he was young. *Sons and Lovers* tells the story of Paul Morel's early family life. Paul's father is a working man, a miner, who drinks too much beer. This is partly because he no longer gets on well with Paul's mother. She turns away from his way of life, looking for better things and wanting to improve the social position of her family. Mrs Morel turns more and more to her four children for comfort. And the children dislike their father, Morel, more and more.

3.7 Identifying the use of the senses

As we have seen, the senses of sight and smell can be important in memory. As you read Text E, notice which of the senses is most important here.

Text E

Paul hated his father. As a boy he had a fervent private religion.
"Make him stop drinking," he prayed every night. "Lord let my father die," he prayed very often. "Let him not be killed at pit," he prayed when, after tea, the father did not come home from work . . .

5   In front of the house was a huge old ash-tree. The west wind, sweeping from Derbyshire, caught the houses with full force, and the tree shrieked again. Morel liked it.
"It's music," he said. "It sends me to sleep."
But Paul and Arthur and Annie hated it. To Paul it became almost
10 a demoniacal noise. The winter of their first year in the new house their father was very bad. The children played in the street, on the edge of the wide, dark valley, until eight o'clock. Then they went to bed. Their mother sat sewing below. Having such a great space in front of the house gave the children a feeling of night, of vastness, and
15 of terror. This terror came in from the shrieking of the tree and the anguish of the home conflicts. Often Paul would wake up, after he had been asleep a long time, aware of thuds downstairs. Instantly he was wide awake. Then he heard the booming shouts of his father, come home nearly drunk, then the sharp replies of his mother, then
20 the bang, bang of his father's fist on the table, and the nasty snarling shout as the man's voice got higher. And then the whole was drowned in a piercing medley of shrieks and cries from the great wind-swept ash-tree. The children lay silent in suspense, waiting for a lull in the wind to hear what their father was doing. He might hit their mother
25 again. There was a feeling of horror, a kind of bristling in the darkness, and a sense of blood. They lay with their hearts in the grip of an intense anguish. The wind came through the tree, fiercer and fiercer. All the cords of the great harp hummed, whistled, shrieked. And then came the horror of the sudden silence, silence everywhere,
30 outside and downstairs. What was it? Was it a silence of blood? What had he done?
The children lay and breathed the darkness. And then, at last, they heard their father throw down his boots and tramp upstairs in his stockinged feet. Still they listened. Then at last, if the wind allowed,

35 they heard the water of the tap drumming into the kettle, which their mother was filling for morning, and they could go to sleep in peace.
   So they were happy in the morning – happy, very happy playing, dancing at night round the lonely lamp-post in the midst of the darkness. But they had one tight place of anxiety in their hearts, one
40 darkness in their eyes, which showed all their lives.

Sons and Lovers, D.H. Lawrence (1913)

Glossary

1 *fervent* : very strong
3 *pit* : coal mine
10 *demoniacal* : wicked or evil, connected with the devil
11 *very bad* : drank a lot and caused trouble
14 *vastness* : a very big space
16 *anguish* : pain and suffering
22 *piercing medley* : very sharp mixture of sounds
23 *lull* : pause
25 *bristling* : a readiness to fight
28 *harp* : a large stringed musical instrument

3.8 Comparing word links

Think again about the words you discussed before reading the text. Find these words in the text and note down what words or ideas they are linked with there. Are any of the links the same as the ones you chose?

3.9 Examining the use of sound words

Sound plays a very important part in Text E. In order to see how Lawrence creates his effect, note down all the words and phrases connected with **sound** or the **absence of sound**.
Work in two sets, A and B. Within the sets, work in pairs. Set A should collect sound words from lines 5–23 and Set B from lines 23–40.
Now complete your list of sound words by asking members of the other set about what they have found.
Are any of the words in your list used more than once in the text?

3.10 Looking at an aspect of mood

Again work in two sets, A and B. Within the sets, work in pairs. Look at the part of the text you did not examine last time.

Set A should collect any **positive** words or ideas.

Set B should collect all words and phrases connected with the **suffering** of the children.

Now ask members of the other set what they have found.

13 *Talk About Literature*

3.11 Discussion

Now that you have looked closely at some of Lawrence's language, you should understand a little about how he creates his effect. What **extra meanings** might be attached to "night" and "morning" in this text?
Do you like the effect Lawrence creates? Do you think he has been successful with his description of the suffering of the Morel children?

Part 4

4.1 Looking at a picture and predicting

Look at the picture. What do you think Text F will be about? What two words, linked frequently with swinging, would you expect to be in the poem? Listen and see if your guesses are correct.

The Golden Gates of Childhood 14

Text F The Swing

    How do you like to go up in a swing,
    Up in the air so blue?
    Oh, I do think it the pleasantest thing
    Ever a child can do!

5   Up in the air and over the wall,
    Till I can see so wide,
    Rivers and trees and cattle and all
    Over the countryside –

    Till I look down on the garden green,
10 Down on the roof so brown –
    Up in the air I go flying again,
    Up in the air and down!

                            R.L. Stevenson (1885)

15 *Talk About Literature*

4.2 Looking at vocabulary

Before you go on to Text G/H, check you know the meaning of the following words taken from it. Work in pairs and use a dictionary if necessary.

> ignore   recognise   separate   hesitate
> apologise   accuse   harm

Text G/H are part of a short story set in Africa. The boy in the story is walking along carrying a bundle of clothes. His mother earns money washing clothes and the boy is delivering the clean clothes back to the house from which they came.

4.3 Summarising

Now read Text G. Without worrying about words you don't know, try to decide what it is about. In pairs, select five or six key words from the text which seem to express the meaning best.
Compare your ideas with the rest of the class.

Text G

He looked longingly at the children on the other side of the railings; the children sliding down the chute, landing with feet astride on the bouncy lawn; screaming as they almost touched the sky with each upward curve of their swings; their joyful, demented shrieks at each
5   dip of the merry-go-round. He looked at them and his body trembled and itched to share their joy – buttocks to fit board, and hands and feet to touch steel. Next to him, on the ground, was a bundle of clothing, washed and ironed, wrapped in a sheet.
  Five small boys, pursued by two bigger ones, ran past, ignoring
10 him. One of the bigger boys stopped. "What are you looking at, you brown ape?" he said, stooping to pick up a lump of clay. He recognised him. The boy was present the day he was put out of the park. The boy pitched the lump, shattering it on the rail above his head and the fragments fell on to his face.
15 He spat out the particles of clay clinging to the lining of his lips, eyes searching for an object to throw at the boys separated from him by the railings. More boys joined the one in front of him and he was frightened by their number.
  Without a word he shook his bundle free from the clay and raised
20 it to his head and walked away.
  As he walked he recalled his last visit to the park. Without hesitation he had gone through the gates and got onto the nearest swing. Even now he could feel that pleasurable thrill which travelled the length of his body as he rocketed himself higher,
25 higher, until he felt that the swing would up-end him when it

reached its peak. Almost leisurely he had allowed it to come to a
halt, like a pendulum shortening its stroke, and then ran towards
the see-saw. A white boy, about his own age, was seated opposite
him. Accordion-like, their legs folded to send the see-saw jerking
30 from the indentation it pounded in the grass. A hand pressing on
his shoulder stopped the jerk. He turned around to look into the
face of the attendant.

"Get off!" The skin tightened between his eyes. "Why must I get
off? What have I done?" He held on, hands clamped on to the iron
35 hoop attached to the wooden see-saw. The white boy jumped off
from the other end and stood – a detached spectator. "You must get
off!" The attendant spoke in a low voice so that it would not carry
to the people who were gathering.

4.4 Predicting what will happen

Why do you think that the boy is being told to get off the see-saw? What do
you think will happen next?

Text H

"The council says," he continued, "that we coloureds must not use
40 the same swings as the whites. You must use the park where you
stay." His voice apologising for the uniform he wore which gave
him the right to be in the park to watch that the little whites were
not hurt while playing.

"There's no park where we stay." He waved a hand in the
45 direction of a block of flats. "There's a park on the other side of
town but I don't know where it is." He walked past them. The
mothers with their babies – pink and belching – cradled in their
arms, the children lolling on the grass, his companion from the see-
saw, the nurse girls – their uniforms their badges of indemnity –
50 pushing prams. Beside him walked another attendant. At the
entrance, the attendant pointed an accusing finger at a
noticeboard.

"There you can read for yourself." Absolving himself from any
blame. He struggled with the red letters on the white background.
55 "Blankes Alleen, Whites Only." He walked through the gates and
behind him swings screeched, the see-saw rattled, and the merry-go-
round rumbled.

He walked past the park as on each occasion after that he had
been forced to walk past it.
60 He shifted the bundle to a more comfortable position, easing the
pain biting into his shoulder muscles. What harm would I be doing
if I were to use the swings? Would it stop the swings from swinging?

17   Talk About Literature

<blockquote>
Would the chute collapse? The bundle pressed deeper and pain became an even line across his shoulders and he had no answer to his reasoning.
</blockquote>

65

From "The Park", James Matthews (1964)

Glossary
- 1   *longingly* : "to long for" means to want something very much
- 3   *bouncy* : soft, almost like rubber
- 11 *lump of clay* : piece of hard mud from the ground
- 30 *indentation* : mark on the ground
- 32 *attendant* : the man who looks after the park
- 45 *block of flats* : large building where people live in apartments
- 49 *badges of indemnity* : signs that the nurse girls were allowed to be in the park although they were black
- 53 *absolving himself from any blame* : showing that the rules of the park were not made by him and he cannot be blamed for them

4.5 Looking at the structure of the story

In pairs, find out which part of the story the boy is remembering and which parts are happening now. Mark where the breaks occur.
Compare your ideas with the class.

4.6 Identifying the sense of touch

In this story, the **touch** or the **feeling** of things is very important. The boy in the story seems to be very sensitive to the feeling of things.
There are two main kinds of feeling which are important to the meaning of the story.
Work in two sets, A and B. Within the sets, work in pairs.

Set A should search lines 1 – 32 for phrases connected with the sense of touch or feeling.
Set B should search lines 33 – 65 for touch or feeling phrases.
An example is "feet on the bouncy lawn".

Write down the phrases and then report what you have found to the class.
Complete your list from what the other set tells you.
What are the two different kinds of feelings?

4.7 Identifying change of mood

In pairs, find the place in the story where the mood changes. Note down the mood words (positive and negative ideas) which best describe the story before the change and after the change.
Look quickly back at the earlier texts in this section. Which text is most similar to Text G/H in its change of mood?

The Golden Gates of Childhood 18

4.8 Searching for words

Work in two sets, A and B. Within the sets, work in pairs.

Set A	Set B
Find the names of four things which are found in a children's playground (first 38 lines). Find two words meaning the same as "small pieces" (lines 9–18).	Find all the words for different kinds of people in the text (e.g. "boys"). Find the phrase which is used to describe the white boy after the two boys are thrown off the see-saw.

Report to the class what you have discovered.

4.9 Discussion

As we have seen, writers sometimes give extra meaning to ordinary things. Try to imagine what extra meaning James Matthews might be giving to the **swing** and to the **bundle of clothes.**
Do you think that the swing in text F has any extra meaning?
Now look back at the photograph on p. 14. Do you think the picture is a good illustration of the text? Do play parks in your country look like this?

Part 5

5.1 Looking at vocabulary

Before you read Text I/J, work in pairs to check you know the meaning of the following words taken from it. Use a dictionary if necessary.

    serious   lie   truth   thief   wicked

As in Text G/H, children can have problems with the adult world but they can also have difficulty with other children.

19 Talk About Literature

Text I/J are part of a play by Dennis Potter, a modern British playwright. The main character is a boy called Nigel Barton. Nigel tells the audience that he has just stolen a daffodil from his classroom and has broken it. He knows he is going to get into serious trouble from the teacher and is very worried.

5.2 Summarising

Listen to the text while you read it. Without worrying about words you don't know, try to get a general idea of what happens in the classroom.

Text I

(*Room is full. Teacher out front. Air of tension and fright*)

MISS TILLINGS: Somebody in this room is a thief! (*Silence*) Somebody – some wicked, wicked child – has stolen our lovely daffodil.
CLASS: Aaah!
5 MISS TILLINGS: Yes, our lovely daffodil. The one we've all watered and tended since the middle of March. Sit absolutely *still* every single one of you. Quite, quite still! I have my own ways of finding nasty little sneak-thieves.
(*A long pause.* MISS TILLINGS *stares hard round the class . . Suddenly*
10 NIGEL *can bear it no longer and his hands go up to his face.*)
MISS TILLINGS: Stand up, Nigel Barton!
(NIGEL *stands, head bowed in shame*)

5.3 Predicting what will happen

Do you think Nigel will be punished for taking the daffodil? Do you think what he has done is serious?

Text J

MISS TILLINGS: Well, Nigel! Do you know anything about this? I can't believe it was you!
15 (*At this last sentence,* NIGEL *looks up, a faint hope glimmering*)
NIGEL: No, Miss.
MISS TILLINGS: Then what do you know about it?
NIGEL: I think I might have had the daffodil, Miss.
MISS TILLINGS (*sharp*): *Might* have had it? What do you mean, boy!
20 Come on, speak up.
NIGEL (*Twisting his head around*): I – I
MISS TILLINGS (*menacingly*): *Well?*
NIGEL: The stem was all broke, Miss. Somebody – somebody – *gave* it to me, Miss.
25 MISS TILLINGS: *Who* gave it to you?
NIGEL: Um. I don't like to say, Miss . . .
MISS TILLINGS: You better had, Barton! And quick about it!

NIGEL: Georgie Pringle, Miss . . .
CLASS: Aaaah!
30 (GEORGIE *jerks up in indignant astonishment*)
PRINGLE: I never did!
MISS TILLINGS: Quiet Pringle! (*She advances on* NIGEL *almost cooing*) All right, Nigel. Thank you. And where did Pringle give you this broken flower?
35 NIGEL: By the bus stop, Miss. The stem was broken. I thought I'd try to mend it.
PRINGLE: It's a lie! A lie!
MISS TILLINGS: You'd better be quiet, Pringle! Does anybody else know anything about this? Did anyone see Pringle with the flower?
40 Anyone see him come back into the school last night?
FIRST BOY: I saw him go back into school, Miss.
PRINGLE: No, Miss! No!
MISS TILLINGS: Quiet! Did you see him come out again?
FIRST BOY: N-no. (*Regretfully*)
45 (*The children sense blood and start to get nasty. There is an air of excitement. Eyes are gleaming.*)
MISS TILLINGS: *Somebody* must have seen him come out again. What about you, Bert. Or are you mixed up in it, too?
BERT (*alarmed*): No, Miss. Not me, Miss.
50 MISS TILLINGS: Well? Was he with you? Did you see him come out? (BERT *is nervous. He shoots a glance at* GEORGIE)
BERT: Y-yes, Miss. He wasn't with me, Miss. I did see him come out, I mean.
(*Class lets out a deep sigh of satisfaction.*)
55 MISS TILLINGS (*quickly*): And he had the daffodil in his hand, didn't he? Didn't he?
BERT: Yes, Miss.
PRINGLE: No, Bert! No!
BERT: In his left hand!
60 GIRL: I saw him too, Miss.
MISS TILLINGS: Where did you see him?
GIRL (*looking round for applause*): By the bread shop, Miss. And he had the daffodil, Miss. The stem was all broke, like Nigel says.
MISS TILLINGS: Come out to the front, Georgie Pringle!
65 PRINGLE (*tearful*): It ent true, none of it, Miss.
MISS TILLINGS: Come out to the front! (*gently*) All right, Nigel, you can sit down now. Thank you for being so truthful.
NIGEL (*smirk*): Thank you, Miss.

Stand Up Nigel Barton, Dennis Potter (1967)

Glossary
30 *indignant astonishment* : surprise and anger
48 *are you mixed up in it* : are you involved, do you have anything to do with it?
65 *ent* : isn't

5.4 Discussion

Do you think children lie more than adults?
Work in pairs and make a list of the reasons why people lie.

5.5 Deciding on the mood of a text

To finish this section, read a song about a child playing.
Which of these words best describes the mood of the text?

happiness   sadness   anger   confusion   worry

Text K Puff the Magic Dragon

Puff the magic dragon lived by the sea,
And frolicked in the Autumn mist in a land called Honalee
Little Jackie Paper loved that rascal Puff
And brought him string and sealing wax and other fancy stuff

Chorus

5   Together they would travel on a boat with billowed sail,
Jackie kept a lookout perched on Puff's gigantic tail,
Noble kings and princes would bow when'ere they came,
Pirate ships would lower their flags when Puff roared out his name.

Chorus

A dragon lives forever but not so little boys.
10 Painted wings and giant's rings make way for other toys
One grey night it happened, Jackie Paper came no more
And Puff that mighty dragon, he ceased his fearless roar.
His head was bent in sorrow, green scales fell like rain
Puff no longer went to play along the cherry lane
15 Without his lifelong friend, Puff could not be brave,
And Puff that mighty dragon sadly slipped into his cave.

Chorus

Peter Yarrow, Paul Lipton (1960's)
(Peter, Paul and Mary)

Glossary
2   *frolicked* : played happily
4   *fancy stuff* : interesting things
7   *when'ere* : whenever
12 *ceased* : stopped
13 *scales* : hard covering of a dragon's skin

5.6 Comparing texts

Look back to the short texts at the beginning of this section. Which of them expresses the opposite to what happens in "Puff"?

5.7 Discussion and survey

If you have read several or all of the texts in this section, find out which of them is most popular and unpopular by taking a vote. Note down how many people vote for each text.
What do you like or dislike about the texts you voted for?

Theme 2 The Happiest Days of Your Life

Part 1

1.1 Deciding about attitudes

Do not worry about the exact meaning of the Introductory Texts. Some difficult words are explained and you can use a dictionary if you wish. Work in pairs and decide which of these texts seems to be **positive** and which seem to be **negative** about school and education.

Text A Introductory Texts

a. The whining schoolboy, with his satchel,
   And shining morning face, creeping like snail
   Unwillingly to school . . .

   As you like it, Shakespeare

b. But, good gracious, you've got to educate him first. You can't expect a boy to be vicious until he's been to a good school.

   Saki

c. (*To the Queen*) I don't know, Madam, why they make all this fuss about education; none of the Pagets [an important family] can read or write, and they get on well enough.

   Lord Melbourne (1779–1848)

d. Schooldays are the happiest days of your life.

   Common saying

e. LADY BRACKNELL: I have always been of the opinion that a man who desires to get married should know either everything or nothing. Which do you know?
   JACK: (*after some hesitation*) I know nothing, Lady Bracknell.
   LADY BRACKNELL: I am very pleased to hear it. I do not approve of anything that tampers with natural ignorance. Ignorance is like a delicate exotic fruit; touch it and the bloom is gone.

   The Importance of Being Ernest, Oscar Wilde

f. If these are the happiest days of your lifes, I recommend mass suicide to you all.

   Lord Brabazon of Tara, Speech to Northampton Boy's Grammar School, 1961

Glossary
whining : complaining
vicious : cruel and unpleasant
tampers with : interferes with
ignorance : the state of knowing nothing
the bloom is gone : it is no longer perfect
suicide : killing oneself

1.2 Making a class survey and discussion

From your own experience, and from what your friends and parents have said, take a class vote on whether you think schooldays are the happiest days of your life.
Now look closely at the classroom and the students in the picture on p. 23. What similarities and differences are there to classroom situations that you know?

1.3 Looking at general vocabulary

In order to read and talk about school and education, it will be useful to know certain words.
Work in two sets, A and B. Within the sets, work in pairs. Check you know the meaning of the following words. Use a dictionary if necessary.

Set A

control
punishment
authority
cooperation
discipline
restriction
fact

Set B

rebellion
younger generation
conflict
respect
behaviour
freedom
imagination

If you do not know the meaning of any of the words in the other list, ask someone in that set.
Discuss in pairs whether there are any other words you think might be useful within the theme of school and education? Look these up in a dictionary and report your ideas to the class.

1.4 Looking at specific vocabulary

The words below are taken from Text B. Work in pairs to check you know their meaning. Use a dictionary if necessary.

calculation   principle   talk somebody into something
reality   ruler   scales

The Happiest Days of Your Life 26

1.5 Matching pictures with text

Listen to Text B and decide which of the pictures below best matches it.

②

③

27 *Talk About Literature*

1.6 Matching descriptions

Now read Text B, which introduces the school teacher in *Hard Times* by Charles Dickens. Try to decide which of the following brief descriptions best matches the character of Thomas Gradgrind.
- A man who is very concerned about his students.
- A man who is very strict and unkind towards his students.
- A man who likes to calculate everything carefully.
- A man of great imagination.

In pairs note down the words and phrases which support your choice. Report your ideas to the class.

Text B

Thomas Gradgrind, sir. A man of realities. A man of facts and calculations. A man who proceeds upon the principle that two and two are four, and nothing over, and who is not to be talked into allowing for anything over. Thomas Gradgrind, sir – peremptorily
5   Thomas – Thomas Gradgrind. With a rule and a pair of scales, and the multiplication table always in his pocket, sir, ready to weigh and measure any parcel of human nature and tell you what it comes to. It is a mere question of figures, a case of simple arithmetic. You may be able to get some other nonsensical belief
10 into the head of George Gradgrind, or Augustus Gradgrind, or John Gradgrind, or Joseph Gradgrind (all suppositions, non-existent persons), but into the head of Thomas Gradgrind – no sir!
    In such terms Mr. Gradgrind always mentally introduced himself, whether to his private circle of acquaintance, or to the public in
15 general.

Glossary
7   *parcel* : detail
9   *nonsensical* : stupid or having no sense
14 *acquaintance* : somebody you know but not a close friend

1.7 Using adjectives for description

Work in sets, A and B. Within the sets, work in pairs.

Set A should make a list of **your own** descriptive words for the kind of teacher Mr Gradgrind ssems to be.

Set B should make a list of descriptive words suitable for the best kind of teacher you can imagine.

Compare your ideas with members of the other set and see if you agree with their choice of adjectives.

pitcher : a large vessel, with handles, for holding liquids
Common saying : Little pitchers have big ears = Children often overhear conversations.

Mr. Gradgrind thinks of his pupils as "little pitchers", which can be filled with facts. Text C describes this filling process. Mr. Gradgrind has two visitors with him in the classroom and wants his class to perform well, as any teacher would.

1.8 Defining objects

Mr Gradgrind wants one of his pupils to give a definition of a horse. Work in pairs to make your own definition of a horse. Also make a definition of one thing you can see in the room you are in.

Example: *Pen* – something you use to write with in ink.

Compare your definitions of a horse. Then read out your other definitions so that others can try to guess the thing you have defined.
Now listen as you read.

Text C

"Girl number twenty," said Mr. Gradgrind, squarely pointing with his square forefinger, "I don't know that girl. Who is that girl?"

"Sissy Jupe, sir," explained number twenty, blushing, standing up, and curtseying.

30   "Sissy is not a name," said Mr. Gradgrind. "Don't call yourself Sissy. Call yourself Cecelia."

"It's Father as calls me Sissy, sir," replied the young girl in a trembling voice, and with another curtsey.

"Then he has no business to do it," said Mr. Gradgrind. "Tell
35   him he mustn't. Cecelia Jupe. Let me see. What is your father?"

"He belongs to the horse-riding, sir." Mr. Gradgrind frowned, and waved off the objectionable calling with his hand. "We don't want to know anything about that here. You mustn't tell us about that, here. Your father breaks horses, don't he?"

40 "If you please, sir, when they can get any to break, they break horses in the ring, sir."

"You mustn't tell us about the ring, here. Very well, then. Describe your father as a horsebreaker. He doctors sick horses, I dare say?"

45 "Oh yes, sir."

"Very well, then. He is a veterinary surgeon, a farrier, and a horsebreaker. Give me your definition of a horse."

(Sissy Jupe thrown into the greatest alarm by this demand.)

"Girl number twenty unable to define a horse!" said Mr.
50 Gradgrind, for the general behoof of all the little pitchers. "Girl number twenty knows no facts in reference to one of the commonest of animals! Some boy's definition of a horse . . . Bitzer," said Thomas Gradgrind. "Your definition of a horse."

"Quadruped. Graminivorous. Forty teeth, namely, twenty-four
55 grinders, four eye-teeth, and twelve incisive. Sheds coat in the spring; in marshy countries, sheds hoofs, too. Hoofs hard, but requiring to be shod with iron. Age known by marks in mouth." Thus (and much more) Bitzer.

"Now girl number twenty," said Mr. Gradgrind. "You know
60 what a horse is."

One of Mr. Gradgrind's visitors now takes over the process of education. He continues on the subject of horses. He asks the pupils if they would decorate a room using wallpaper which had pictures of horses upon it. Before reading further, decide whether you would use horse wallpaper to decorate a room. And would you buy a carpet which had a pattern of flowers on it? What are your reasons?

Text D

"Very well," said this gentleman, briskly smiling, and folding his arms. "That's a horse. Now, let me ask you girls and boys: Would you paper a room with representations of horses?"

After a pause, one half of the children shouted in chorus, "Yes,
65 sir!" Upon which the other half, seeing in the gentleman's face that Yes was wrong, cried out in chorus, "No, sir!" – as the custom is in these examinations.

"Of course, No. Why wouldn't you?"

A pause. One corpulent slow boy, with a wheezy manner of
70 breathing, ventured the answer, because he wouldn't paper a room at all, he would paint it.

"You *must* paper it," said the gentleman, rather warmly.

"You must paper it," said Thomas Gradgrind, "whether you like

it or not. Don't tell *us* you wouldn't paper it. What do you mean,
75 boy?"
"I'll explain to you, then," said the gentleman, after another and a dismal pause, "why you wouldn't paper a room with representations of horses. Do you ever see horses walking up and down the sides of rooms in reality – in fact? Do you?"
80 "Yes sir!" from one half of the class. "No, sir!" from the other.
"Of course, No," said the gentleman, with an angry look at the wrong half. "Why, then, you are not to see anywhere what you don't see in fact; you are not to have anywhere what you don't have in fact. What is called Taste is only another name for Fact."
85 Thomas Gradgrind nodded his approbation. "This is a new principle, a discovery, a great discovery," said the gentleman. "Now, I'll try you again. Suppose you were going to carpet a room. Would you use a carpet having a representation of flowers upon it?"
90 There being a general conviction by this time that "No, sir!" was always the right answer to this gentleman, the chorus of No was very strong. Only a few feeble stragglers said Yes: among them Sissy Jupe.
"Girl number twenty," said the gentleman, smiling in the calm
95 strength of knowledge.
Sissy blushed, and stood up.
"So you would carpet your room – or your husband's room, if you were a grown woman, and had a husband – with representations of flowers, would you?" said the gentleman. "Why
100 would you?"

1.9 Replying to a question

Imagine you are in Sissy's class. Consider what your answer might be to the gentleman's question. Work in pairs and think of as many suitable replies as you can.
Then listen to and read Text E.

Text E

"If you please sir, I am very fond of flowers," returned the girl.
"And is that why you would put tables and chairs on them, and have people walking over them with heavy boots?"
"It woudn't hurt them, sir. They wouldn't crush and wither, if
105 you please sir. They would be the pictures of what was very pretty and pleasant, and I would fancy —"
"Yes, yes, yes! But you mustn't fancy," cried the gentleman, quite elated by coming so happily to his point. "That's it! You are never to fancy."

110   "You are not, Cecilia Jupe," Thomas Gradgrind solemnly repeated, "to do anything of that kind."

"Fact, fact, fact!" said the gentleman. And "Fact, fact, fact!" repeated Thomas Gradgrind.

Hard Times, Charles Dickens (1854)

Glossary

28   *blushing* : going red in the face from embarrassment
29   *curtseying* : an old-fashioned way for girls to show respect; men bowed and women curtseyed
34   *has no business to do it* : ought not to do it
39   *breaks horses* : trains horses to be ridden
54   *graminivorous* : eats grass
57   *shod* : have iron shoes put on them
63   *representations* : pictures or shapes
72   *warmly* : getting slightly angry
84   *Taste* : having taste means being able to select the best and the most beautiful in art and design
85   *approbation* : approval and agreement
104   *crush* : get damaged or flattened
106   *fancy* : imagine

1.10 Giving a title

Which of these titles do you think Dickens used for this chapter of *Hard Times*? (Texts B–E)

A Typical Day at School   Filling the Little Pitchers
Murdering the Innocents   Facts and Definitions

1.11 Matching diagram to text

Decide which of these diagrams best shows the relationship between student and teacher in the Dickens text.

(5)

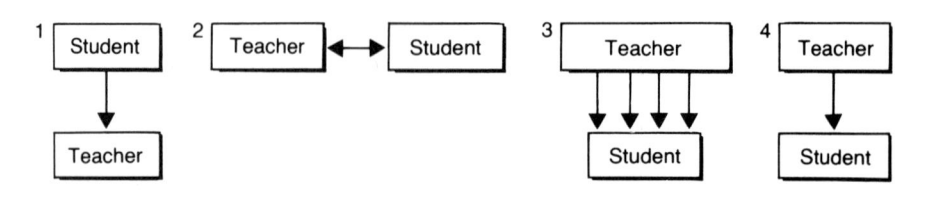

1. Student → Teacher
2. Teacher ↔ Student
3. Teacher → → → → Student
4. Teacher → Student

Which do you think is the best relationship? Is this possible?

1.12 Word sorting and discussion

Work in pairs. Sort this list of words into two columns according to how they seem to link together.

>art	fact	mechanical	doubt	freedom
>certainty	science	imagination	creative	control

One pair should write the two columns on the blackboard to compare with the rest of the class.
Which of these columns best describes the situation in Texts B–E?

Part 2

2.1 Looking at vocabulary

Before you go on to Text F, look at some of the words from this poem. Work in pairs to check their meaning and use a dictionary if necessary.

>summer	sweet	cruel	sigh	anxious
>delight	cage	joy	shower	annoy

Does this group of words give you an idea of the mood of the poem?

2.2 Listening and summarising

Text F is a poem by William Blake called "The Schoolboy". It was written more than fifty years before *Hard Times* (Texts B–E).

Now listen to the poem while you follow the text.
Then work in pairs to decide what you think Blake is saying about school.

Text F The Schoolboy

>I love to rise in a summer morn
>When the birds sing on every tree;
>The distant huntsman winds his horn
>And the skylark sings with me.
>5 O! What sweet company.
>
>But to go to school in a summer morn,
>O! it drives all joy away;
>Under a cruel eye outworn,
>The little ones spend the day
>10 In sighing and dismay
>
>Ah! then at times I drooping sit,
>And spend many an anxious hour,
>Nor in my book can I take delight,
>Nor sit in learning's bower,
>15 Worn through with the dreary shower.

How can the bird that is born for joy
Sit in a cage and sing?
How can a child, when fears annoy,
But droop his tender wing,
20 And forget his youthful spring?

O! father and mother, if buds are nipped
And blossoms blown away,
And if the tender plants are stripped
Of their joy in the springing day,
25 By sorrow and care's dismay,

How shall the summer arise in joy,
Or the summer fruits appear?
Or how shall we gather what griefs destroy,
Or bless the mellowing year,
30 When the blasts of winter appear?

William Blake (1794)

Glossary
3   *winds* : blows
8   *outworn* : worn out
10 *dismay* : being filled with discouragement
11 *drooping* : hanging down in an unhappy way
14 *learning's bower* : a poetic name for school or a quiet place where learning can take place
21 *nipped* : broken off
22 *blossoms* : flowers on a tree
29 *mellowing* : getting ripe. Applied to the year, this indicates the season of Autumn in Britain
30 *blasts* : strong winds

2.3 Listening to a discussion

Work in two sets, A and B. Within the sets, work in pairs.

Set A should look for:
Where the schoolboy is in the 1st verse.
What the schoolboy is compared to in the 6th verse.
Where the schoolboy is in the 2nd verse.

Set B should look for:
What the schoolboy is compared to in the 4th verse.
Who or what is "cruel" in the 2nd verse.
What the schoolboy is compared to in the 5th verse.

In order to help you discover this information and understand the poem more clearly, you can listen to the discussion about the poem between a teacher and two students (Tapescript 1, p.109).
When you have found the information you need, ask members of the other set what they have discovered about the poem.

The Happiest Days of Your Life 34

2.4 Supporting an opinion

"This poem is about the destruction of childhood joy."

Decide what you think about this statement. To help you do this, work in pairs to make two lists, one containing all the positive words or ideas you can find in the poem and the other containing the negative words and ideas.
Which is the longer of the two lists? What does this tell you about the meaning of the poem?

2.5 Discussion

Is Blake's description of school anything like your own experience?
In pairs, make a list of the **freedoms** and the **restrictions** you have experienced at school. Compare your ideas with the class.
Are the restrictions necessary?

2.6 Discussion

The rock group Pink Floyd made a record and a film called *The Wall* which, like Blake's poem, are concerned with the loss of freedom. *The Wall* is about a rock singer called Pink. Pink's childhood was very unhappy and he did not like his experience at school. He feels that his education is a brick in the wall of restriction which now surrounds him. The chorus of one of the songs in *The Wall* includes the words, "We don't need no education, we don't need no thought control". Education is rejected here because it is seen as limiting freedom and controlling thoughts.
Do you feel that the ideas you learn or learned in school are useful or do you feel your own ideas could not develop? Is your education a brick in a wall which imprisons you or does it free you to think for yourself?

2.7 Reading for specific information

Read a song about education.
As you read, note down any of the things which the person in the song learns in school.
Then compare what you have found with the rest of the class.

Text G What did you learn in school today?

Chorus:
What did you learn in school today
Dear little boy of mine?
What did you learn in school today
Dear little boy of mine?

I learned that Washington never told a lie
I learned that soldiers never die
I learned that everybody's free
And that's what the teacher said to me
And that's what I learned in school today
That's what I learned in school

Chorus

I learned that policemen are my friends
I learned that justice never ends
I learned that murderers die for their crimes
Even if we make a mistake sometimes
And that's what I learned in school today
That's what I learned in school

Chorus

I learned that war is not so bad
I learned about the great ones we have had
We fought in Germany and in France
And someday I might get my chance
That's what I learned in school today
That's what I learned in school

Chorus

I learned our government must be strong
It's always right and never wrong
Our leaders are the finest men
And we elect them again and again
And that's what I learned in school today
That's what I learned in school

Tom Paxton (1960's)

2.8 Checking and discussion

Read the song again to check what you have listed. Also try to decide whether Tom Paxton's ideas are similar or different to those of Blake and of Pink Floyd.

Part 3

Discipline is kept in schools by punishments of different kinds. Physical, or corporal, punishment was still used in British schools until fairly recently. Text H shows an example of punishment in a large English school in the 1950's.

3.1 Looking at vocabulary

Before you read Text H, check you know the meaning of the following words taken from it. Work in two sets, A and B. Within the sets, work in pairs. Match the words with the explanations below.

Set A
junk
encounter
deceitful
get away with

Set B
handle (verb)
inspect
distaste
panic (noun)

- a feeling of suddenly being very frightened
- control and look after
- not telling the truth
- a feeling that something is unpleasant
- meet, come across
- worthless things, rubbish
- not be caught
- look closely at

Now ask members of the other set if they know the meaning of the words you have looked up. Tell them the meanings if they don't.

Now, in pairs, note down any ideas the words in both lists are often linked with. For example, "panic" might be associated with darkness.

In Text H, three boys are about to be punished for smoking in school. While they are waiting outside the headmaster's room, another boy arrives to bring a message from a teacher. The three smokers persuade this messenger to hide their cigarettes and matches in his pockets. In this way they hope to escape more trouble. The four boys are then brought into the headmaster's room together.

Text H

"I've taught in this city for over thirty-five years now; many of your parents were pupils under me in the old city schools before this estate was built; and I'm certain that in all those years I've never encountered a generation as difficult to handle as this one. I thought I understood young people, I should be able to with all my experience, yet there's something happening today that's frightening, that makes me feel it's all been a waste of time . . .

"So for want of a better solution I continue using the cane, knowing full well that you'll be back time and time again for some more. Knowing that when you smokers leave this room wringing your hands, you'll carry on smoking just the same. Yes, you can smirk, lad. I'll bet your pockets are ladened up at this very moment in readiness for break; aren't they? Aren't they? Well just empty them. Come on, all of you empty your pockets!"

15   The three smokers began to reveal their collected paraphernalia. The messenger watched them in panic, the colour rising in his face like the warming bar of an electric fire. He stepped forward again.

"Please, Sir . . ."

"Quiet lad! And get your pockets emptied!"

20   The lad's face cooled to the colour of dripping as he began to empty his pockets. Gryce moved along the line, broddling in their palms; turning and inspecting the grubby contents with obvious distaste.

"This can't be true. I don't believe it."

25   He placed his stick on the desk.

"Keep your hands out."

And started down the line again, frisking their clothing quickly and expertly. When he reached the messenger he beamed at him.

"Ah! Ah!"

30   "Please, Sir . . ."

The smokers leaned forward and looked at him, half turning and angling across each other like a prioll of Jacks. They squared their jaws and showed him their teeth. Tears came into the messenger's eyes and he began to snuffle.

35   "You're a regular cigarette factory aren't you, lad?"

From various pockets Gryce collected two ten-packets, which rattled when he shook them, a handful of tabs, three lighters and a box of matches.

"You deceitful boy. You didn't think you could get away with
40   such a weak trick, did you?"

He strode over to the basket at the side of his desk and dropped the lot into it.

"Now get that other junk back into your pockets, and get your hands out."

45   He picked his stick up from his desk and tested it on the air. The first smoker stepped out and raised his right hand. He proffered it slightly cupped, thumb tucked into the side, the flesh of the palm ruttled up into soft cushions.

Gryce measured the distance with the tip of his stick, settled his
50   feet, then slowly flexed his elbow. When his fist was level with his ear, the hinge flashed open swish down across the boy's palm. The boy blinked and held up his left hand. The stick touched it, curved up and away out of Gryce's peripheral vision, then blurred back into it and snapped down across the fingers.

55   "Right, now get out."

White-faced, he turned away from Gryce, and winked at the others as he passed in front of them to the door.

"Next."

They stepped forward in turn, all adopting the same relaxed
60   hand position as the first boy. Except for the messenger. He presented his hands stiff, fingers splayed, thumbs up. The full force

The Happiest Days of Your Life 38

of both strokes caught him thumbs first, cracking across the side of the knuckle bone. The first stroke made him cry. The second made him sick.

A Kestrel for a Knave, Barry Hines (1968)

Glossary

3 *estate* : housing estate, area of new and cheap houses for poorer people
12 *smirk* : smile in a self-satisfied way
12 *ladened up* : full up
13 *break* : morning and lunch-time pause between lessons
15 *paraphernalia* : bits and pieces in their pockets
20 *dripping* : fat
21 *broddling* (local dialect) : pushing the objects around
22 *with obvious distaste* : clearly disliking what he was doing
32 *prioll of Jacks* : row of playing cards

3.2 Comparing word associations

Think again about the words you discussed before reading the text. Find these words in the text and note down what words or ideas they are linked with there. Are any of the links the same as the ones you chose?

3.3 Matching pictures with text

Find the lines in the text which match these pictures.

3.4 Matching sentences with text

Work in two sets, A and B. Within the sets, work in pairs. Find the lines in the text which match the sentences below.

Set A

a) He held his hand in such a way that the soft parts were showing.

b) I don't think I have ever met a set of students who are so hard to control.

Set B

a) The boys who had been smoking looked at the messenger in a threatening way.

b) Because I don't have a better answer to the problem, I have to keep punishing you like this although I know perfectly well you'll be back many, many times.

Report what you have found to the class.

3.5 Retelling the story

Work in pairs and note down very briefly the main points about what happens in the text. You can begin:

Headmaster talks to students about their crime . . .

Discuss your ideas with the class.

3.6 Comparing texts

If you have already worked through the first section of this book, "The Golden Gates", look back and see if you can find a text there which contains a similar idea to Text H in this section.

3.7 Discussion

Take a class vote on whether physical punishment should be used at all in schools. Then vote on whether punishment should be used at all in schools.

In pairs make a list of the kinds of misbehaviour which occur in schools. Then list suitable types of punishment for this misbehaviour.
Report your ideas to the class.

The Happiest Days of Your Life 40

Part 4

Now compare what happens to a child who misbehaves in a very different situation.

Laurie Lee, the author of Text I/J, went to a small country school. None of the children like the head teacher, who they call Crabby B. She rushes into the classroom in the morning and immediately begins to find fault with the pupils. She punishes them for reasons they don't understand.

4.1 Finding out what happens

A boy called Spadge Hopkins decides to fight back against the unpleasant teacher. As you listen and read, don't worry about details. Simply try to find out what Spadge does when the teacher tells him what to do.

Text I

Spadge Hopkins it was, and I must say we were surprised. He was one of those heavy, full-grown boys, thick-legged, red-fisted, bursting with flesh, designed for the great outdoors. He was nearly fourteen by then, and physically out of scale – at least so far as our
5   school was concerned. The sight of him squeezed into his tiny desk was worse than a bullock in ballet-shoes. He wasn't much of a scholar; he groaned as he worked or hacked at his desk with a jack-knife. Miss B took her pleasure in goading him, in forcing him to read out loud; or asking him sudden unintelligible questions
10 which made him flush and stumble.

The great day came; a day of shimmering summer, with the valley outside in a state of leafy levitation. Crabby B was at her sourest, and Spadge Hopkins had had enough. He began to writhe in his desk, and roll his eyes, and kick with his boots, and mutter;
15 "She'd better look out. Her, – Crabby B. She'd better, that's all. I can tell you . . ."

We didn't quite know what the matter was, in spite of his meaning looks. Then he threw down his pen, said; "Sod it all," got up, and walked to the door.
20 "And where are you going, young man, may I ask?" said Crabby with her awful leer.

Spadge paused and looked her straight in the eye.

"If it's any business of yourn."

We shivered with pleasure at this defiance, Spadge leisurely made
25 for the door.

"Sit down this instant!" Crabby suddenly screamed. "I won't have it!"

"Ta-ta," said Spadge.

Then Crabby sprang like a yellow cat, spitting and clawing with
30 rage. She caught Spadge in the doorway and fell upon him. There was a shameful moment of heavy breathing and scuffling, while the

teacher tore at his clothes. Spadge caught her hands in his great red fists and held her at arm's length, struggling.

"Come and help me, someone!" wailed Crabby, demented. But
35 nobody moved; we just watched. We saw Spadge lift her up and place her on the top of the cupboard, then walk out of the door and away. There was a moment of silence, then we all laid down our pens and began to stamp on the floor in unison. Crabby stayed where she was, on top of the cupboard, drumming her heels and
40 weeping.

Glossary
3   *great outdoors* : open space
4   *out of scale* : too big
6   *bullock* : young bull
8   *goading* : tormenting
13   *sourest* : most unpleasant
13   *writhe* : twist about uncomfortably
21   *leer* : unpleasant smile
23   *If it's any business of yourn* : if it's got anything to do with you. Spadge means that the teacher has no right to ask him where he is going
24   *defiance* : rebellion
28   *ta-ta* : good bye
31   *scuffling* : fighting
34   *demented* : in a mad way
38   *in unison* : at the same time

4.2 Predicting what will happen

What do you think the teacher did about the class and about Spadge after she was put on top of the cupboard? Work in pairs and think of what might happen. Report your ideas to the class.

Text J

We expected some terrible retribution to follow, but nothing happened at all. Not even the trouble-spark, Spadge, was called to account – he was simply left alone. From that day Crabby never spoke to him, or crossed his path, or denied him anything at all. He
45 perched idly in his desk, his knees up to his chin, whistling in a world of his own. Sometimes Miss B would consider him narrowly and if he caught her glance he just winked. Otherwise he was free to come and go, and to take time off as he pleased.

Cider with Rosie, Laurie Lee (1959)

Glossary
41   *retribution* : punishment
42   *called to account* : punished
44   *crossed his path* : went near him
44   *denied him* : said he couldn't have
46   *consider him narrowly* : look closely at him

4.3 Looking at the language of description

Find out how Laurie Lee's language creates a lively effect. One way he does this is to make comparisons.
If an author lives in the country, what will he probably compare things with? Work in two sets, A and B. Within the sets, work in pairs. Look for certain details.

Set A	Set B
Find out what Spadge Hopkins is compared to and note down the words and phrases used to describe him.	Find out what Crabby B is compared to and note down the words and phrases used to describe her.

4.4 Comparing texts

In pairs note down all the similarities and differences you can find between Texts H and I/J. For example, both texts are set in school, but one of them has a male headteacher and the other has a female headteacher.

4.5 Looking at vocabulary

Before you go on to the last text in this section, check you know the meaning of the following words from this text. Work in two sets, A and B. Within the sets, work in pairs.

Set A	Set B
essay	imagination
test	detention
inspiration	rubbish

Ask members of the other set if you don't know the meaning of any of their words.

4.6 Listening for the main idea

Text K is a poem which gives another example of rebellion in the classroom. The poem was written by a 13-year-old girl.
Listen to the poem and try to find out **who** is the main voice in the poem and **what** the children do when they rebel against the teacher.

Text K The Essay

My mouth twitching,
Slowly I parade the room,
Full of 2D, shifting uneasily
In their seats.

5   This is no test,
Just an ordinary lesson
With, of course, an essay.
One of my best, if I do say so myself –
The Adventures of Blank the Snail.

10 Only one person in the
Whole room is writing.
The rest sit, chewing their pens,
Hoping for inspiration.

As I walk slowly round them
15 Killing all their imagination,
A small girl with a blue ribbon
Says to me, "Sir, I'm not writing this."
I pause, place myself in a
Position to tower over her
20 And begin, "And why not . . .?"

"I'm . . . I'm sorry, Sir,
But this is a
Load of Rubbish."
She gets up to go.

25 "A detention, a detention,"
I shriek.
The whole class walks out.
I am left with
Half an essay and 31 titles.

30 The power of my word is gone.
The icicles at my
Fingertips have melted.

Ellen Jackson (1987)

Glossary
1   *twitching* : moving nervously
3   *2D* : a second year class
19 *tower over her* : being very large beside her
25 *detention* : a punishment, keeping children in school after the last lesson

4.7 Comparing texts

Look back at the diagrams on page 31. Which lines in "The Essay" matches one of those diagrams?

4.8 Discussion

Work in pairs to discuss why you like or dislike "The Essay".
If you were writing a poem about school, what things would you put in it?
List the positive or negative things you would mention.
Compare your ideas with the rest of the class.

4.9 Review and survey

If you have read most or all of the texts in this section, look back to find those which are most similar in subject to "The Essay". Which other teacher is most like the one here?
Now find out if the easiest text in this section is also the most popular. Take a class vote. Which text do you like most? Which text do you find easiest to read?

Theme 3 All Work and No Play

Part 1

①

Working for a living is something most people have to do at some time.

1.1 Class survey

Take a class vote. How many people really enjoy work and how many people would rather **not** work if they had the choice?

1.2 Deciding about attitudes

In pairs look quickly through the following short texts and decide which authors seem to think that work is a good idea and which do not like it so much.

Text A Introductory Texts

a. All work and no play makes Jack a dull boy.

Proverb

b. He observed, that labouring men who work hard, and live sparingly, are seldom or never troubled with low spirits.

Life of Johnson, James Boswell

c. It always seems to me that I am doing more work than I should do. It is not that I object to work, mind you; I like work; it fascinates me. I can sit and look at it for hours.

Three Men in a Boat, Jerome K. Jerome

d. Consider the lilies, how they grow; they toil not, neither do they spin: And yet I say unto you, That even Solomon in all his glory was not arrayed like one of these.

The Bible

e. Blessed is he who has found his work; let him ask no other blessedness.

Thomas Carlyle

f. What is this life if, full of care
We have no time to stand and stare.

W.H. Davies

Glossary
dull : not lively, probably boring
low spirits : unhappiness or depression
sparingly : economically, simply
toil : work
arrayed : clothed

1.3 Looking at vocabulary

The following words will be useful when you are reading and talking about work. Check you know their meaning. Work in two sets, A and B. Within the sets, work in pairs. Use a dictionary if necessary.

Set A

labour
idle (ness)
amateur
leisure
career
independence

Set B

industrious
lazy
professional
employment
beggar
livelihood

Ask members of the other set if you do not know the meaning of any of their words.

1.4 Discussing pictures

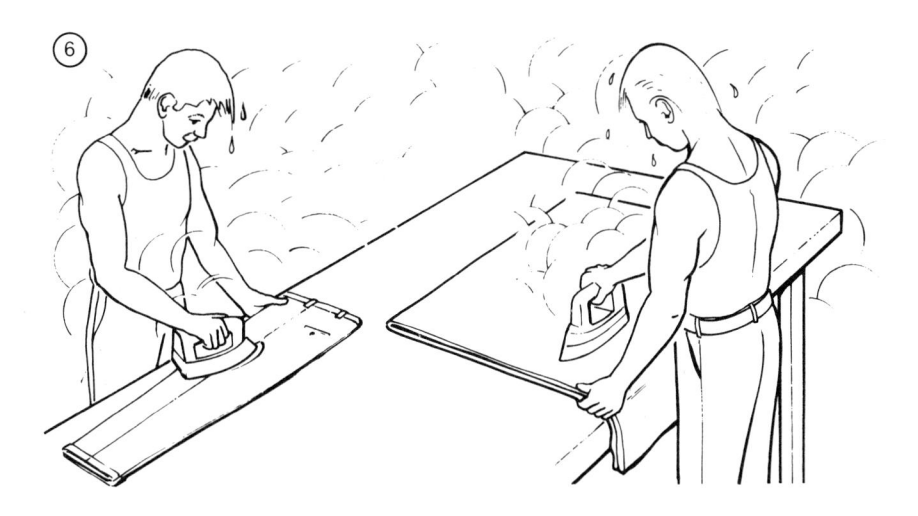

All Work and No Play 48

⑥

In pairs discuss what you think is happening in each of the pictures.
Report to the class your suggestions about the pictures and compare these ideas.

1.5 Matching pictures with text

Again work in pairs and try to match your pictures with the texts in this section. Quickly glance through the whole section, and do not worry about details. Simply try to find a text which seems to fit with the pictures you have been looking at.
Report your ideas to the class.

1.6 Listening for general meaning

Now listen to the first text, which is a translation of a Chinese poem. Try to decide which of the Introductory Texts is closest to it in meaning. Note down any words which you think are important.

Text B Lazy Man's Song

    I could have a job, but I am too lazy to choose it;
    I have got land, but am too lazy to farm it.
    My house leaks; I am too lazy to mend it.
    My clothes are torn; I am too lazy to darn them.
5   I have got wine, but am too lazy to drink;
    So it's just the same as if my cup were empty.
    I have got a lute, but am too lazy to play;
    So it's just the same as if it had no strings.
    My family tells me there is no more steamed rice;

10 I want to cook, but am too lazy to grind.
My friends and relatives write me long letters;
I should like to read them, but they're such a bother to open.
I have always been told that Hsi Shu-yeh
Passed his whole life in absolute idleness.
15 But he played his lute and sometimes worked at his forge;
So even *he* was not so lazy as I.

Po Chu-i, A.D. 811, translated by Arthur Waley

Glossary
7   *lute* : musical instrument with strings
14 *absolute* : complete
15 *forge* : where metal things are made

1.7 Discussion

In pairs, make a list of all the things that the man in the poem does not want to do.
Can you believe this man is so lazy? Which things are hardest to believe?

Part 2

The next two texts are taken from a novel called *Martin Eden* by Jack London. Martin Eden, who is a portrait of Jack London himself, had little education at school but has fallen in love with a rich girl, Ruth, who is now going to university. Hoping to be able to marry her, he starts trying to educate himself. He begins to read many books and to write articles and stories for magazines. In this way he hopes to earn enough money, and to be educated enough, to be able to marry Ruth.

2.1 Looking at vocabulary

Before you go on to Text C/D, look at these words which have been taken from it. Match the words with the explanations below. Work in pairs and use a dictionary if necessary.

experiment   pursuit   automatic   accuracy   sever   exhausting
        consolation   unconsciousness   hell

- _____ is when you take great care and make no mistakes
- the state of not being aware of what is happening
- a very unpleasant hot place
- very tiring
- an activity or something you do
- something done like a machine or with no thought is _____
- something which makes up for, or compensates for, something bad
- doing something you have never done before
- to cut

2.2 Making a summary

Work in two sets, A and B. Within the sets, work in pairs. Set A should look at Text C on page 50 and set B at Text D on page 52.
Do not worry about the meaning of specific words, but try to make a very short summary of what the text is about. Tell members of the other set about the kind of work described in your text.

2.3 Finding specific information

Now everyone should look in more detail at Text C. Again work in two sets, A and B. Within the sets, work in pairs.

| Set A should make a list of any phrases which show whether Martin Eden likes or dislikes his work. | Set B should list the different activities which are mentioned in the text. |

Ask members of the other set about what they have found and make a note of what they tell you.

Text C

Following the 'Pearl-Diving', he wrote an article on the sea as a career, another on turtle-catching, and a third on the north-east trades. Then he tried, as an experiment, a short story, and before he broke his stride he had finished six short stories, and sent them
5   to various magazines. He wrote prolifically, intensely, from morning to night, and late at night, except when he broke off to go to the reading-room, draw books from the library, or to call on Ruth. He was profoundly happy. Life was pitched high. He was in a fever that never broke. The joy of creation that is supposed to have
10   belonged to the gods was his. All the life about him, the odours of stale vegetables and washing, the slatternly form of his sister, and the jeering face of Mr. Higginbotham, was a dream. The real world was in his mind, and the stories he wrote were so many pieces of reality out of his mind.
15   The days were too short. There was so much he wanted to study. He cut his sleep down to five hours, and found that he could get along upon it. He tried four hours and a half, and regretfully came back to five. He could joyfully have spent all his waking hours upon any one of his pursuits. It was with regret that he ceased from
20   writing to study, that he ceased from study to go to the library, that he tore himself away from that chart-room of knowledge or from the magazines in the reading-room that were filled with the secrets of writers who succeeded in selling their wares. It was like severing

51 *Talk About Literature*

heart-strings, when he was with Ruth, to stand up and go; and he
25 scorched through the dark streets so as to get home to his books at the least possible expense of time. And hardest of all was to shut up the algebra or physics, put the notebook and pencil aside, and close his tired eyes in sleep. He hated the thought of ceasing to live, even for so short a time, and his only consolation was that the alarm-
30 clock was set five hours ahead. He would lose only five hours, anyway, and then the jangling bell would jerk him out of unconsciousness, and he would have before him another glorious day of nineteen hours.

Glossary
4   *broke his stride* : slowed down
5   *prolifically* : great amount
8   *pitched high* : very exciting
11 *slatternly form* : untidy appearance
12 *jeering* : laughing unkindly at
25 *scorched* : normally means burn but here means to run at great speed
29 *consolation* : comfort

2.4 Looking at language and vocabulary

Writers often do not use the simplest words to express their ideas. Instead of the simple word "stop", in the sense of "stop doing something", Jack London uses several phrases to mean the same thing.
Work in two sets, A and B. Within the sets, work in pairs.

Set A should try to make a list of all the phrases in the text which mean "stop doing something".

Set B should try to match the following simplified phrases with the ones London actually uses.

Simplified phrases: a) left the library, b) the noisy alarm clock would wake him up, c) he went quickly home at night to save time, d) he found it hard to leave Ruth.

Report what you have found to the class.

2.5 Class survey: sleep analysis

Do you need the same amount of sleep as Martin or do you require more? Find out how much sleep each person in the class requires and draw a bar chart to show the different amounts. Use the same kind of diagram as this one based on sleep requirements of students in a language class in England.

All Work and No Play 52

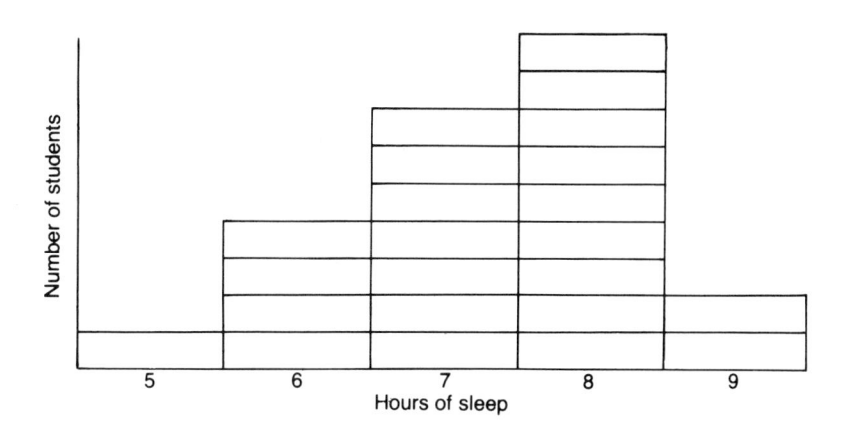

Martin Eden thought that sleep was "ceasing to live". Do you think sleep is a waste of time and would you like to sleep less? If you slept less, what would you do with the extra time?

2.6 Reading and noting

Later in the book, Martin is faced with another kind of work. He is forced to take a job because he has no money left to buy food or to post his manuscripts to the magazines.
Read Text D and in pairs note down all words and phrases which describe how difficult and unpleasant Martin's work is.

Text D

It was exhausting work, carried on, hour after hour, at top speed. Out on the broad verandas of the hotel men and women, in cool white, sipped iced drinks and kept their circulation down. But in the laundry the air was sizzling. The huge stove roared red hot and
5 white hot, while the irons, moving over the damp cloth, sent up clouds of steam. The heat of the irons was different from that used by housewives. An iron that stood the ordinary test of a wet finger was too cold for Joe and Martin, and such test was useless. They went wholly by holding the irons close to their cheeks, gauging the
10 heat by some secret mental process that Martin admired but could not understand. When the fresh irons proved too hot, they hooked them on iron rods and dipped them into cold water. This, again, required a precise and subtle judgement. A fraction of a second too long in the water, and the proper heat was lost; and Martin found
15 time to marvel at the accuracy he developed – an automatic accuracy, founded upon criteria that were machine-like and unerring.

But there was little time in which to marvel. All Martin's consciousness was concentrated in the work. There was no room in his brain for the universe and its mighty problems . . . The cool guests on the verandas needed clean linen.

The sweat poured from Martin. He drank enormous quantities of water, but so great was the heat of the day and of his exertions that the water sluiced through the intersices of his flesh and out at all his pores. Always, at sea, except at rare intervals, the work he performed had given him ample opportunity to commune with himself. The master of the ship had been lord of Martin's time; but here the manager of the hotel was lord of Martin's thoughts as well. He had no thoughts save for the nerve-racking, body-destroying toil. Outside of that, it was impossible to think. He did not know that he loved Ruth. She did not even exist, for his driven soul had no time to remember her. It was only when he crawled into bed at night, or to breakfast in the morning, that she asserted herself to him in fleeting memories.

'This is hell, ain't it?' Joe remarked once.

Martin nodded, but felt a rasp of irritation. The statement had been obvious and unnecessary. They did not talk while they worked. Conversation threw them out of their stride, as it did this time, compelling Martin to miss a stroke of his iron and to make two extra motions before he caught his stride again.

Martin Eden, Jack London (1909)

Glossary

3 *circulation* : movement of blood in the body
4 *sizzling* : extremely hot, frying
5 *irons* : tools to press clothes
9 *gauging* : judging
17 *unerring* : without any mistakes
23 *exertions* : great efforts
26 *commune with himself* : think
38 *threw out of their stride* : interrupted the smoothness of their work

2.7 Comparing ideas

Work in pairs to discuss the difference between the kinds of work described in Text C/D. Consider Martin's reaction to these different kinds of work. Have you ever had similar work experiences to these?

Part 3

3.1 Class survey: your favourite day of the week

Make a class survey about your favourite day of the week. One student can call out each day of the week in turn and the rest of the class raise their hands when their favourite day is named. Note down the number of votes for each day.
Then give reasons for your choice.
Can you draw any conclusions from your survey?

3.2 Listening

Listen to Text E. This text is about a young man called Arthur Seaton. Don't worry about what you don't understand but try to find out three things while you are listening:
a) What Arthur Seaton's favourite day is.
b) Why he likes this particular day.
c) What kind of work Arthur Seaton does.
Compare your ideas with a partner and then read the text to see if you are right.

Text E

He lifted a pair of clean overalls from the bed-rail and pulled them over his big white feet, taking care not to disturb his brother Sam who, while still in the depths of sleep, rolled himself more advantageously into the large mound of blankets now that Arthur
5 had left the bed. He had often heard Friday described as Black Friday – remembering a Boris Karloff film of years ago – and wondered why this should be. For Friday, being pay-day, was a good day, and 'black' would be more fitting if applied to Monday. Black Monday. Then there would be some sense in it, when you felt
10 your head big from boozing, throat sore from singing, eyes fogged-up from seeing too many films or sitting in front of the television, and feeling black and wicked because the big grind was starting all over again . . .
 The minute you stepped out of the factory gates you thought no
15 more about your work. But the funniest thing was that neither did you think about work when you were standing at your machine. You began the day by cutting and drilling steel cylinders with care, but gradually your actions became automatic and you forgot all about the machine and the quick working of your arms and hands
20 and the fact that you were cutting and boring and rough-threading to within limits of only five-thousandths of an inch. The noise of motor-trolleys passing up and down the gangway and the excruciating din of flying and flapping belts slipped out of your

consciousness after perhaps half an hour, without affecting the
quality of the work you were turning out, and you forgot your past
conflicts with the gaffer and turned to thinking of pleasant events
that had at some time happened to you, or things that you hoped
would happen to you in the future. If your machine was working
well – the motor smooth, stops tight, jigs good – and you spring
your actions into a favourable rhythm you became happy. You
went off into pipe-dreams for the rest of the day. And in the
evening, when admittedly you would be feeling as though your arms
and legs had been stretched to breaking point on a torture-rack,
you stepped out into a cosy world of pubs and noisy tarts that
would one day provide you with the raw material for more pipe-
dreams as you stood at your lathe.

Saturday Night and Sunday Morning, Alan Sillitoe (1958)

Glossary
1   *overalls* : working clothing made in one piece
10 *boozing* : drinking
12 *big grind* : the working week
31 *pipe-dreams* : fantasies, imaginary situations
34 *tarts* : girls (slang)
35 *raw material* : ideas

3.3 Guessing meanings

Find the words below in the text and try to guess their meanings using the clues on the right to help you.

fogged-up	What are the effects on your eyes of watching too much TV?
excruciating din	A difficult phrase, but what would you expect the environment in a factory to be like?
the gaffer	Who would Arthur Seaton be likely to have conflicts or arguments with at work?

3.4 Identifying words that are not important

A number of words in Text E are connected with the work Arthur Seaton does. There are a number of **verbs** which are linked with the working of the machines and there are a number of **nouns** which are the names of machines or parts of machine. It is **not** necessary to understand the meaning of these words but it is useful to be able to identify them.

Work in two sets, A and B. Within the set, work in pairs.

Set A should look for the verbs linked with the working of machines.
Note down these words.

Set B should look for the names of machines or parts of machines.
Note down these words.

Report to the class what you have discovered.

3.5 Discussion: comparing types of work

Martin Eden in Text D was soon forced to give up his work in the laundry. Arthur Seaton is able to continue with his work in the factory. He finally gets married while he is still employed there.
Why do you think Martin had to stop work but Arthur could continue?

3.6 Thinking about questions people ask

When strangers meet, on a train for example, they might begin to ask each other questions. Work in pairs and write down the first **five** questions you think they would probably ask each other.
Compare your ideas with the rest of the class. How many pairs listed "What's your job?" or "What do you do for a living?".
Is a person's job the most important thing in his or her life? If not, what **is** most important?

3.7 Listening

First look at the list of words taken from a poem by D.H. Lawrence.

leisured classes : people who don't have to work for a living
carpenter : someone who makes things from wood
joiner : maker of furniture
thrush : a common, brown garden bird in Britain
flautist : someone who plays a flute
quibble : to argue about small and unimportant points

There are two speakers in the poem. First listen to the poem and try to find out what they are discussing.
Compare your idea with the rest of the class and then read the poem to check your first impression.

Text F What is he?

    What is he?
    – A man, of course.
    Yes, but what does he do?
    – He lives and is a man.
5   Oh quite! but he must work. He must have a job of some sort.
    – Why?
    Because obviously he's not one of the leisured classes.
    – I don't know. He has lots of leisure. And he makes quite beautiful chairs.
10   There you are then! He's a cabinet maker.
    – No no!
    Anyhow a carpenter and a joiner.

57 Talk About Literature

```
              - Not at all.
              But you said so.
         15   - What did I say?
              That he made chairs, and was a joiner and a carpenter.
              - I said he made chairs, but I did not say he was a carpenter.
              All right then, he's just an amateur.
              - Perhaps! Would you say a thrush was a professional flautist, or
         20   just an amateur?
              I'd say it was just a bird.
              - And I say he is just a man.
              All right! You always did quibble.
```
D.H. Lawrence (1929)

Part 4

4.1 Discussion

Philip Larkin is a modern British poet. In his poem "Toads", Larkin does not seem to like work. He compares the idea of work to an animal sitting heavily on his life. If **you** compared work to an animal, which animal would you choose?

This is what Larkin wrote at the beginning of "Toads".

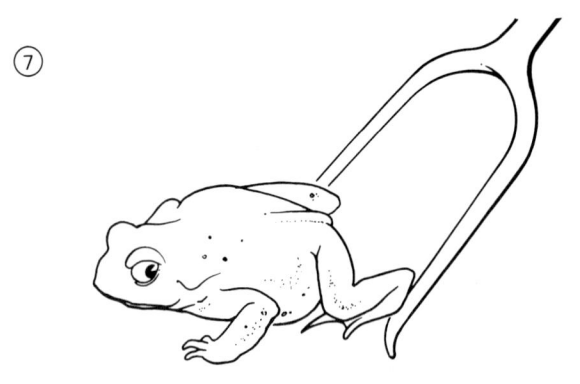

⑦

```
     Why should I let the toad work
     Squat on my life?
     Can't I use my wit as a pitchfork
     And drive the brute off?

5    Six days of the week it soils
     With its sickening poison -
     Just for paying a few bills!
     It's out of proportion.
```

Glossary
3 *wit* : intelligence, perhaps humour too
4 *brute* : a negative word for an animal
5 *soils* : makes dirty

Having a sense of proportion means keeping things in balance, not doing too much of one thing and too little of another. Larkin feels he does too much work just to pay his bills.

4.2 Looking at vocabulary

Before you read Text G work in pairs to check that you know the meaning of these words. Use a dictionary if necessary.

acquire	expenses	income	maintain
hardship	pastime	luxury	interrupt

4.3 Predicting ideas

Henry David Thoreau was an American who also wrote about the idea of proportion in work. He thought most people worked far too much. Thoreau decided to try to live very cheaply close to nature and he built himself a small hut in the woods in Concord, Massachusetts. He did not want to be linked with a "job", as in the D.H. Lawrence poem.
Thoreau thought that free time, when you can do exactly what you want, is very important. Make a guess about how much time he thought he needed to work each year in order to make a living.
What do you think he did with his free time?

Text G

For more than five years I maintained myself thus solely by the labour of my hands, and I found that, by working about six weeks in a year, I could meet all the expenses of living. The whole of my winters, as well as most of my summers, I had free and clear for
5   study. I have thoroughly tried school-teaching, and found my expenses were in proportion, or rather out of proportion, to my income, for I was obliged to dress and train, not to say think and believe, accordingly, and I lost my time into the bargain. As I did not teach for the good of my fellow-men, but simply for a
10   livelihood, this was a failure . . .
  As I preferred some things to others, and especially valued my freedom, I did not wish to spend my time in earning rich carpets or other fine furniture, or delicate cookery, or a house in the Grecian or Gothic style just yet. If there are any to whom it is no
15   interruption to acquire these things, and who know how to use them when acquired, I relinquish to them the pursuit. Some are "industrious", and appear to love labour for its own sake, or perhaps because it keeps them out of worse mischief; to such I have at present nothing to say . . .
20   For myself I found that the occupation of a day-labourer was the

most independent of any, especially as it required only thirty or forty days in a year to support one. The labourer's day ends with the going down of the sun, and he is then free to devote himself to his chosen pursuit, independent of his labour; but his employer, who speculates from month to month, has no respite from one end of the year to the other.

In short, I am convinced, both by faith and experience, that to maintain one's self on this earth is not a hardship but a pastime, if we will live simply and wisely . . . It is not necessary that a man should earn his living by the sweat of his brow, unless he sweats easier than I do.

Walden, Henry David Thoreau (1854)

Glossary

7   *train* : prepare for, learn the skills of something
16 *relinquish* : give up
25 *speculate* : invest money to try to make more
25 *respite* : rest or relief

4.4 Searching for a word

Look back to the list of words in 4.2. One word in this list is not actually used in the text. Thoreau does give examples of this word, however. Work in pairs to check the text to find the word and the examples which are given of it.

4.5 Discussion about ways of living

Work in two sets, A and B. Within the sets, work in pairs.

Set A should discuss whether it would be possible to work only six weeks a year. Would you like this kind of life and what sort of work could you do?

Set B should discuss whether it would be worth giving up all luxuries in order to make time and freedom for yourself. What luxuries would you be prepared to do without?

Discuss your ideas with the class.

4.6 Finding the general meaning

Now you can listen to and read a complete poem by Philip Larkin. In this poem, Larkin goes back to his comparison of work with a toad. We saw that in "Toads" he wanted to escape from work, like Throeau.
Try to find out whether Larkin says he accepts or rejects the idea of work.

Text H Toads Revisited

Walking around in the park
Should feel better than work:
The lake, the sunshine,
The grass to lie on,

5   Blurred playground noises
Beyond black-stockinged nurses –
Not a bad place to be.
Yet it doesn't suit me.

Being one of the men
10 You meet of an afternoon:
Palsied old step-takers,
Hare-eyed clerks with the jitters,

Waxed-fleshed out-patients
Still vague from accidents,
15 And characters in long coats
Deep in the litter-baskets –

All dodging the toad work
By being stupid or weak.
Think of being them!
20 Hearing the hours chime,

Watching the bread delivered,
The sun by clouds covered,
The children going home;
Think of being them,

25 Turning over their failures
By some bed of lobelias,
Nowhere to go but indoors,
No friend but empty chairs –

No, give me my in-tray,
30 My loaf-haired secretary,
My shall-I-keep-the-call-in-Sir:
What else can I answer,

When the lights come on at four
At the end of another year?
35   Give me your arm, old toad;
Help me down Cemetery Road.

Philip Larkin (1964)

Glossary

5   *blurred* : not clear
11 *palsied old step-takers* : helpless, pathetic old people for whom even walking is difficult
12 *hare* : like a rabbit, but larger
12 *jitters* : nervousness
13 *wax* : what candles are made of
13 *out-patients* : people who have to visit a hospital for treatment but who do not stay overnight
17 *dodging* : escaping
25 *turning over* : thinking about
26 *lobelia* : a type of flower
36 *cemetery* : place where people are buried

4.7 Matching pictures with text

In pairs look at the pictures of the different people who are mentioned in the poem.

Find the lines in the poem which match the pictures above. There is one person described in the poem who has no picture. Which one is that?

4.8 Finding ideas by reading and listening to a discussion

Listen to a teacher talking about "Toads Revisited" with three students in order to help you find the following ideas in the poem (Tapescript 2, p. 109). Work in two sets, A and B. Within the sets, work in pairs. Look for the following:

Set A

What the speaker of the poem does for a living.
What the speaker feels about his job.

Set B

The meaning of Cemetery Road.
The five things the people in the park are doing.

Read Tapescript 2 if you wish. Then ask members of the other set to see if they know the answers to what you have been looking for. Tell them if they can't answer your questions.

Part 5

Text I is about a very different and rather unusual kind of work.

5.1 Discussion

What do you think of beggars? Do you consider that what beggars do can be called work?
In pairs note down **five** adjectives which you link with the idea of beggars. Compare your ideas with the rest of the class.

5.2 Looking at vocabulary

Before you go on to the text, check you know the meaning of the following words which are taken from it. Work in two sets, A and B. Within the sets, work in pairs. Use a dictionary if necessary.

Set A	Set B
despise	reputable
respectable	outcast
worthless	profitable

Ask members of the other set if you do not know the meaning of any of their words.

Text I

People seem to feel that there is some essential difference between beggars and ordinary "working" men. They are a race apart – outcasts, like criminals and prostitutes. Working men "work", beggars do not "work"; they are parasites, worthless in their very nature. It is taken for granted that a beggar does not "earn" his living, as a bricklayer or a literary critic "earns" his . . .

Yet if one looks closely one sees that there is no *essential* difference between a beggar's livelihood and that of numberless respectable people. Beggars do not work, it is said; but, then, what is *work*? A navvy works by swinging a pick. An accountant works by adding up figures. A beggar works by standing out of doors in all weathers and getting varicose veins, chronic bronchitis, etc. It is a trade like any other; quite useless, of course – but, then, many reputable trades are quite useless . . .

Then the question arises, Why are beggars despised? – for they are despised, universally. I believe it is for the simple reason that they fail to earn a decent living. In practice, nobody cares whether work is useful or useless, productive or parasitic; the sole thing demanded is that it shall be profitable.

Down and out in Paris and London, George Orwell (1933)

Glossary
2 *a race apart*: a different kind of person
4 *parasites* : people or animals which live off others

5.3 Discussion

Orwell makes a number of statements about beggars.

He says that begging is a trade or a job like any other.
He says that beggars are disliked because they do not make a decent or respectable living.

Do you agree with these opinions?

5.4 Class survey

Take a class vote about giving money to beggars. If a beggar comes up to you in the street and asks for money, would you give:

never   sometimes   always

5.5 Discussion

Think about this statement concerning work:

> There is no point in work
> unless it absorbs you
> like an absorbing game.
>
> If it doesn't absorb you
> 5   if it's never any fun
> don't do it

D.H. Lawrence

Glossary
2   *absorb* : completely involve, greatly interest

Is it really possible to think like this about your work? Is it possible always to be interested in work?
What kind of work **do** you consider is fun?

5.6 Selecting a text

Look quickly back through the texts you have read in this section.
Which of them best expresses your own feelings about work? Is this the same as the text you enjoyed most?

Theme 4 The Root of All Evil

Part 1

①

For many people, money is one of the most important things in their lives, perhaps the most important thing.

1.1 Deciding about attitudes

Work in pairs to look at the Introductory Texts and decide which of them take a **positive** view of money and which take a **negative** view.

Text A Introductory Texts

a. If you would be perfect, go and sell all you have, and give to the poor, and you shall have treasure in heaven.

b. It is easier for a camel to go through the eye of a needle, than for a rich man to enter into the kingdom of God.

The Bible

c. Money is the most important thing in the world. It represents health, strength, honour, generosity and beauty as conspicuously and undeniably as the want of it represents illness, weakness, disgrace, meanness and ugliness.

Preface to *Major Barbara*, George Bernard Shaw

d. I'm tired of Love; I'm still more tired of Rhyme,
But Money gives me pleasure all the time.

Hilaire Belloc

e. In my experience, I have found nothing so truly impoverishing as what is called wealth.

H.D. Thoreau

f. There are few ways in which a man can be more innocently employed than in getting money.

Samuel Johnson

g. Those who hoard up gold and silver and do not spend it in the cause of Allah will be punished. The day will surely come when their treasures shall be heated in the fire of Hell, and their foreheads, sides, and backs burned with them.

The Koran

Glossary
conspicuously : noticeably, obviously
want : lack
impoverishing : when something makes you poorer
hoard : save more than you need

1.2 Discussion

First look back to the Introductory Texts of "The Golden Gates" section on pages 1 and 2. Try to find which of those texts says that something is more valuable than money.
Work in pairs and make a list of the things which **you** think are more important or valuable than money.
Compare your ideas with the rest of the class.

1.3 Suggesting words

Now work in pairs once again and note down **ten** words or ideas you connect with money – getting money, spending money, saving money or losing money. Use a dictionary if you wish.
Compare your suggestions with the rest of the class and make a list of the most important words or ideas on the board.

1.4 Extending vocabulary

In order to read and talk about the subject of money, it will also be useful to know the words in the following list. Some of these words you may have already suggested.
Work in two sets, A and B. Within the sets, work in pairs. Check you know the meaning of these words and use a dictionary if necessary.

Set A	Set B
miser	wealth
afford	luxury
poverty	expenditure
necessity	waste (verb)
materialism	credit (noun)
status	mean (adj)

Ask members of other sets if you do not know the meaning of any words in their list.

1.5 Discussion

People often say, "Money is the root of all evil", meaning that all bad things are caused by money.
Do you agree with this statement? Do you think this is a good title for this section in the book?
In pairs make a list of the bad things and the good things which you feel that money can do.
In fact when people say "Money is the root of all evil", they are quoting wrongly from *The Bible*, where we find:

"The **love of money** is the root of all evil"

1.6 Class survey

Make a list of the first five things you would do or buy if you had as much money as you wanted. Compare your list with the class and write on the board those things which five or more people have mentioned.

The Root of All Evil 68

How many of the things you have listed can be found in the pictures below? Did you think of anything which is *not* illustrated here?

1.7 Discussion

In English there is the expression "Keeping up with the Joneses". This refers to the habit people have of trying to keep up with their neighbours in status. So, if your neighbour (perhaps called Jones) buys a better car, then you might want to improve your car as well. If your neighbour gets a video recorder, then you might feel you need to get one too.
Is there an expression in your language which means the same as "Keeping up with the Joneses"? Do you think that people actually buy things because their neighbour or someone they know has got them? Can you think of any times when you have seen this happen?

Part 2

> I am a millionaire. That is my religion.
>
> Undershaft in *Major Barbara*, G.B. Shaw
>
> – Who wants to be a millionaire?
> – I don't, 'cause all I want is you.
>
> Song from the film *High Society*

A miser, as you have discovered, is someone who loves to save or hoard money and who dislikes spending any. The most famous miser in English literature is Scrooge in *A Christmas Carol* by Charles Dickens. In fact, the word "scrooge" is still used today about people who are mean with their money.

2.1 Looking at vocabulary

Before you go on to Texts B, C and D, which are about a miser, match the following words from the texts with the definitions below. Work in two sets, A and B. Within the sets, work in pairs.

Set A

accumulate
conscious
monotonous
satisfaction

Set B

solitary
passion
wander
imprisonment

- a very deep interest
- walk along in an unhurried way
- being aware of or knowing about something
- gather together or collect
- being all alone
- pleasure about something
- when activity is the same all the time it is _____
- the state of being shut up and unable to get out

Now ask members of the other set if they know the meaning of the words you have looked up. Tell them the meanings if they can't answer your questions.

George Eliot (who was actually a woman) wrote a book called *Silas Marner* about a miser. Eliot describes how Silas begins to save money and to love collecting it.

Silas is a weaver or maker of cloth. At the beginning of the book, he is a simple and honest man, who is very interested in religion. He earns money but gives most of it away to charity. However, he is accused of a robbery he did not do and is driven away from his home. He moves south to a small village called Raveloe and there he continues to make his living as a weaver. He lives alone and only meets the village people when he does work for them. He earns quite a lot of money with his weaving but now has no use for it, no charity to give it to. There is nothing he wants to buy.

⑦

2.2 Collecting key words

Now read Text B fairly quickly and when you have done so note down in pairs five words which you think are most important to the meaning of the text. Then compare your list with the rest of the class.

Text B

Gradually the guineas, the crowns, and the half-crowns grew to a heap, and Marner used less and less for his own wants, trying to solve the problem of keeping himself strong enough to work sixteen hours a day on as small an outlay as possible . . . the love of
5   accumulating money grows into an absorbing passion in men whose imaginations showed them no purpose beyond the money itself. Marner wanted the heaps of ten to grow into a square, and then into a larger square; and every added guinea, while it was itself a

10 satisfaction, bred a new desire . . . He began to think his money was conscious of him, as his loom was, and he would on no account have exchanged those coins, which had become his familiars, for other coins with unknown faces. He handled them, he counted them, till their form and colour were like the satisfaction of a thirst to him; but it was only in the night, when his work was done, that
15 he took them out to enjoy their companionship. He had taken up some bricks in his floor underneath his loom, and here he had made a hole in which he put the iron pot that contained his guineas and silver coins. He covered the bricks with sand whenever he replaced them. Not that the idea of being robbed came into his mind clearly
20 or often . . .

The livelong day he sat in his loom, his ear filled with its monotony, his eyes bent close down on the slow growth of the sameness in the brownish web, his muscles moving with such even repetition their pause seemed almost as much a constraint as the
25 holding of his breath. But at night came his revelry: at night he closed his shutters, and made fast his doors, and drew out his gold. Long ago the heap of coins had become too large for the iron pot to hold them, and he had made for them two thick leather bags, which wasted no room in their resting place. How the guineas shone
30 as they came pouring out of the dark leather mouths! . . . He spread them out in heaps and bathed his hands in them; then he counted them and set them up in regular piles, and felt their rounded outline between his thumb and fingers, and thought fondly of the guineas that were only half-earned by the work in his loom,
35 as if they had been unborn children – thought of the guineas that were coming slowly through the coming years, through all his life, which spread far away before him, the end quite hidden by countless days of weaving. No wonder his thoughts were still with his loom and his money when he made his journeys through the
40 fields and the lanes to fetch and carry home his work, so that his steps never wandered to the hedge banks and the lane side in search of the once familiar herbs: these too belonged to the past, from which his life had shrunk away, like a rivulet that has sunk far down from the grassy fringe of its old breadth into a little
45 shivering thread, that cuts a groove for itself in the barren sand.

Glossary

1 *guinea* : gold coin
1 *crown, half crown* : silver coins
4 *outlay* : the money you spend to live
5 *absorbing passion* : a great interest which takes up a lot of time
10 *loom* : machine for making cloth
15 *companionship* : company or friendship
23 *brownish web* : the cloth Silas is weaving
25 *revelry* : celebration, relaxation and excitement
26 *shutters* : wooden coverings for windows
43 *rivulet* : river

2.3 Finding ideas in the texts

Work in two sets, A and B. Within the sets, work in pairs. Find the following things in the text.

Set A

Find anything in the text which shows that Silas treats his money as if it were **human**.

Set B

Silas's life is getting narrower and smaller through his growing interest in money. Eliot compares this process to something else getting smaller. Find this comparison.

Which lines in the text most closely match the picture above the text?

Report what you have found to the class.

2.4 Finding out how word pictures are created

Try to find out how Eliot builds up her picture of Silas Marner the miser. To do this, in pairs note down all the words and phrases connected with money and Silas' love of it. Underline those words which contain an 's' sound or any other soft sound. "Guineas" is an example.
Do you think the word picture Eliot makes of Silas is a good, clear one? Does the sound of the words help at all in making this picture clear?

2.5 Predicting what will happen

First read the following short summary of how the story develops.

In Raveloe also lived a rich Squire or landowner. This man had two sons, Dunstan and his older brother Godfrey. Both of them were in great need of money. Dunstan knew that Silas Marner was rich and wondered if he could borrow some money from the weaver. He knew also that Silas would probably not wish to lend any money. Instead Dunstan persuaded Godfrey to let him sell his horse. Dunstan was riding this horse when it fell and was killed. Dunstan found himself alone in the countryside, carrying only his brother's whip. By chance he came near Silas Marner's cottage. It was getting dark and foggy and Dunstan thought he could borrow a light from Silas. He also thought he could try to borrow some money while he was there. Dunstan knocked on the cottage door. There was no answer. Dunstan pushed the door and found to his surprise that it was not locked.

73 Talk About Literature

In pairs discuss what you think Dunstan does now. Compare your ideas with the rest of the class and then continue reading to see if any of these ideas are the same as the story.

Text C

But where could he be at this time, and on such an evening, leaving his door unfastened? Dunstan's own recent difficulty in making his way suggested to him that the weaver had perhaps gone outside his cottage to fetch in fuel, or for some such brief purpose, and had
50 slipped into the Stone Pit. That was an interesting idea to Dunstan, carrying consequences of entire novelty. If the weaver was dead, who had a right to his money? Who would know where his money was hidden? *Who would know that anybody had come to take it away?* He went no further into the subtleties of evidence: the pressing
55 question, "Where is the money?" now took such entire possession of him as to make him quite forget that the weaver's death was not a certainty . . . There were only three hiding places where he had ever heard of cottagers' hoards being found: the thatch, the bed, and a hole in the floor. Marner's cottage had no thatch; and
60 Dunstan's first act, after a train of thought made rapid by the stimulus of cupidity, was to go up to the bed; but while he did so, his eyes travelled eagerly over the floor, where the bricks, distinct in the firelight, were discernable under the sprinkling of sand. But not everywhere; for there was one spot, and one only, which was quite
65 covered with sand, and sand showing the marks of fingers which had apparently been careful to spread it over a given space. It was near the treadles of the loom. In an instant Dunstan darted to that spot, swept away the sand with his whip, and, inserting the thin end of the hook between the bricks, found that they were loose.

Glossary
50 *Stone Pit* : a deep hole in the ground where stone had been dug out in the past
58 *thatch* : roof of a house made of straw
60 *after a train of thought . . . .* : after his thoughts were made rapid by his greed
62 *distinct* : very clear, very easily visible
63 *discernible* : noticeable

2.6 Predicting what will happen

Work in pairs and note down your ideas about what might happen next. Compare your ideas with the rest of the class and then continue reading.

Text D

70 In haste he lifted up two bricks, and saw what he had no doubt was the object of his search: for what could there be but money in those two leather bags? And from their weight, they must be filled with guineas. Dunstan felt round the hole, to be certain that it held no more; then hastily replaced the bricks, and spread the sand over
75 them. Hardly more than five minutes had passed since he entered the cottage, but it seemed to Dunstan like a long while: and though he was without any distinct recognition of the possibility that Marner might be alive, and might re-enter the cottage at any moment, he felt an undefinable dread laying hold on him, as he
80 rose to his feet with the bags in his hand. He would hasten out into the darkness, and then consider what he should do with the bags. He closed the door behind him immediately, that he might shut in the stream of light . . . The rain and darkness had got thicker, and he was glad of it; though it was awkward walking with both hands
85 filled, so that it was as much as he could do to grasp his whip along with one of the bags. But when he had gone a yard or two, he might take his time. So he stepped forward into the darkness.

Silas Marner, George Eliot (1861)

Glossary
71 *the object of his search* : what he was looking for
77 *without any distinct recognition* : without any clear idea
79 *undefinable dread* : a fear of an unknown kind

Silas Marner was not of course dead. He returned to his cottage a short time later and almost went mad when he found that his long-saved money was gone, even though he had no particular need for it.

2.7 Class discussion

There is an English proverb:

"A fool and his money are soon parted."

Do you think Silas Marner was a fool?

2.8 Deciding on the mood of a text

Text E shows a very different attitude to robbery. This is a Buddhist story about how a monk behaves towards a thief who comes to steal his few possessions. Listen first to the text and try to decide which of the following words best describes its mood.

happiness   anger   sadness   worry   humour   confusion

Then read the text to check your first impression.

Text E   The Moon Cannot Be Stolen

A Buddhist monk once lived in a small hut at the foot of a mountain. He lived a simple life and had very few possessions. But any kind of house attracts thieves and one day a thief came to the monk's small hut. He wondered what he might find inside and went
5   up to the door. He looked through the door and discovered that the monk was not there. "What luck!" he thought and went quickly into the hut. There was only one room and so he could see very soon that there was nothing at all he could steal. There were only one or two pots, a mat on the floor and some flowers.
10   He was standing angrily in the hut trying to think of what to do next when the monk returned and caught him in the room. "You have probably come a long way to visit me here," said the monk with a smile, "and you should not return home empty-handed. I have not got very much to offer, but please accept my clothes as a
15   present."
The thief was very confused by this. He took the clothes from the monk and crept away shaking his head in surprise.
Later that evening, the monk sat naked on his mat looking up at the moon and thinking of the thief. "Poor man," he said aloud. "I
20   wish I could give him this beautiful moon."

2.9 Comparing texts

Work in two sets, A and B. Within the sets, work in pairs.

Set A should note down anything which is similar between the texts in Part 2 and set B should note down the differences.
Ask members of the other set questions about the similarities or differences they have discovered.

The Root of All Evil 76

Part 3

3.1 Looking at vocabulary

Text F/G gives another example of greed but comes from a different continent. Before you read the texts, check you know the meaning of the following words taken from them. Work in two sets A and B. Within the sets, work in pairs. Use a dictionary if necessary.

Set A

sinister
disappointment
nervous
opportunity
cattle
retreat
consciousness

Set B

undecided
foolish
echo
hesitate
search
pocket
idiot

Ask members of the other set if they know the meaning of the words you have discussed. Tell them the meaning if they can't answer your questions.

3.2 Predicting what will happen

In pairs discuss what you can guess about Text F/G from looking at the picture and from the words you have checked. Where is the story set and what do you think it is about? Compare your ideas with the class and then read the introduction below.

77 *Talk About Literature*

Grace Ogot, a Kenyan writer, wrote a story in which some cattle thieves are discovered trying to take some bulls from a small village. The thieves are chased in the night by the villagers. The thieves miss a bridge over a river, and one of them is caught. He is badly beaten and covered with a pile of green leaves. The villagers leave him to die and intend to come back to deal with the body in the morning. Nyagar, one of the villagers, returns to his hut after the chase.

3.3 Discussion

Somebody in the story says:

"Don't deceive yourself that you have enough wealth.
Nobody in the world has enough wealth."

Who do you imagine says this in the story?
Do you agree with the statement?
Now listen while you read the first part of the text.

Text F

He sat on the end of his bed. He started to remove his clothes. Then he changed his mind. Instead he just sat there, staring vacantly into space. Finally he made up his mind to go back to the dead man alone.

5   He opened the door slowly, and then closed it quietly after him. No one must hear him.

He did not hesitate at the gate, but walked blindly on.

"Did I close the gate?" he wondered. He looked back. Yes, he had closed it – or it looked closed.

10 Apart from a sinister sound which occasionally rolled through the night, everything was silent. Dawn must have been approaching. The faint and golden gleams of light that usually herald the birth of a new day could be seen in the east shooting skywards from the bowels of the earth. "He must have a lot of money in his pocket,"
15 Nyagar said aloud. He knew that stock thieves sold stolen cattle at the earliest opportunity.

"The others were foolish not to have searched him." He stopped and listened. Was somebody coming? No. He was merely hearing the echo of his own footsteps.

20 "Perhaps the other two thieves who had escaped are now back at the scene," he thought nervously. "No, they can't be there – they wouldn't be such idiots as to hang around there."

The heap of green leaves came into sight. A numb paralysing
pain ran through his spine. He thought his heart had stopped
25   beating. He stopped to check. It was still beating, all right. He was
just nervous. He moved on faster, and the echo of his footsteps
bothered him.
   When Nyagar reached the scene of the murder, he noticed that
everything was exactly as they had left it earlier. He stood there for
30   a while, undecided. He looked in all directions to ensure that no
one was coming. There was nobody. He was all alone with the
dead body. He now felt nervous. "Why should you disturb a dead
body?" his inner voice asked him. "What do you want to do with
money? You have three wives and twelve children. You have many
35   cattle and enough food. What more do you want?" the voice
persisted.

Glossary
12   *herald* : announce
14   *bowels* : deepest parts
15   *stock* : cattle
24   *spine* : backbone
27   *bothered* : disturbed or worried
30   *ensure* : make certain
35   *the voice persisted* : the voice inside him kept on speaking

3.4   Looking at vocabulary

Look at these three words.

   blind   vacant   paralysed

Work in pairs to note down what you usually link with these words – what
other words are often found with them?
Then look back at Text F to see how they are used there. Are they used in
the way you noted? Why do you think these words have been chosen?

3.5   Finding out how a person is described

Work in two sets, A and B. Within the sets, work in pairs.

Set A should look at lines 1 – 19 of   Set B should look at lines 20 – 36 of
the text and note down all the   the text and note down all the
words and phrases which are used   words and phrases which are used
to describe how Nyagar feels.   to describe how Nyagar feels.

Report to the class what you have discovered.

3.6 Predicting what will happen

What do you think Nyagar decides to do? What would **you** do if you were in his position? Discuss your ideas with the class.

Now listen first to Text G without reading to try to find out what **does** happen.

Text G

He felt even more nervous, and was about to retreat when an urge stronger than his will egged him on.

"You have come all this far for one cause only, and the man is lying before you. You only need to put your hand in his pockets, and all the money will be yours. Don't deceive yourself that you have enough wealth. Nobody in the world has enough wealth."

Nyagar bent over the dead man, and hurriedly removed the leaves from him. His hand came in contact with the man's arm which lay folded on his chest. It was still warm. A chill ran through him again, and he stood up. It was unusual for a dead person to be warm, he thought. However, he dismissed the thought. Perhaps he was just nervous and was imagining things. He bent over the man again, and rolled him on his back. He looked dead all right.

He fumbled quickly to find the pockets. He dipped his hand into the first pocket. It was empty. He searched the second pocket – that, too, was empty. A pang of disappointment ran through his heart. Then he remembered that cattle traders often carried their money in a small bag stringed with a cord around their neck.

He knelt beside the dead man and found his neck. Sure enough there was a string tied round his neck, from which hung a little bag. A triumphant smile played at the corner of his mouth. Since he had no knife with which to cut the string, he decided to remove it over the man's head. As Nyagar lifted the man's head, there was a crashing blow on his right eye. He staggered a few yards and fell unconscious to the ground.

The Root of All Evil 80

              The thief had just regained consciousness and was still very weak. But there was no time to lose. He managed to get up on his feet after a second attempt. His body was soaked in blood, but his
65   mind was now clear. He gathered all the green leaves and heaped them on Nyagar. He then made for the bridge which he had failed to locate during the battle.

"The Green Leaves", Grace Ogot (1985)

Glossary
38   *egged him on* : encouraged him
45   *chill* : cold feeling
47   *dismissed the thought* : stopped thinking about it

Nyagar was in fact killed by the cattle thief. The other villagers were of course astonished to find their friend beneath the pile of leaves when they went back next morning.

Part 4

4.1 Reading and finding words

Text H is a song which shows another aspect of the love of money and what it can buy.
Read the song and note down all the words connected with money.

Text H   Material Girl

Some boys hate me, some boys hug me
I think they're OK
If they don't give me proper credit
I just walk away-ay
5   They can beg and they can plead but
They can't see the light (that's right!)
Because the boy with the cold hard cash
Is always Mr Right

Chorus:
'Cos we are living in a material world
10   And I am a material girl
You know that we are living in a material world
And I am a material girl

Some boys roam and some boys know
That's alright with me
15   If they can't pay my interest
Then I have to let them be

Some boys try and some boys lie but
I don't let them play (no way!)
Only boys that save their pennies
20   Make my rainy day-ay

Chorus

Boys may come and boys may go and
That's alright you see
Experience has made me rich and
Now they're after me

Chorus

Recorded by Madonna (1980's)

Glossary

3   *credit* : money on loan, thus credit cards are used to buy things without cash
15 *interest* : the charge made for borrowing money. If the interest rate is high, you have to pay a lot extra for a loan

4.2 Discussion

Does this picture of the modern young woman seem to you to be correct? Do you think young people today are more materialistic than they used to be?

4.3 Reading for general meaning

Text I is about an ambitious young man starting out in life. Joe Lampton has a new job at the local council offices in Duffton. He is not paid very much and he finds the life rather dull.
He enters a cafe and suddenly feels very conscious of everything around him. He sees himself as if he were in a film, with every detail of his surroundings very clear to him. He takes a seat near the window and orders some tea. Suddenly he sees something that "changes his whole life".
Don't worry about any details you can't understand. Try to find out what changed Joe Lampton's life. What does he suddenly know that he wants?

Text I

Parked by a solicitor's office opposite the cafe was a green Aston-Martin tourer, low-slung, with cycle-type mudguards. It had the tough, functional smartness of the good British sports car; . . . it wasn't the sort of vehicle for business or for family outings but quite
5   simply a rich man's toy.
    As I was admiring it a young man and a girl came out of the solicitor's office. The young man was turning the ignition key when

the girl said something to him and after a moment's argument he put up the windscreen . . .

10   The ownership of the Aston-Martin automatically placed the young man in a social class far above mine; but that ownership was simply a question of money. The girl, with her even suntan and her fair hair cut short in a style too simple to be anything but expensive, was as far beyond my reach as the car. But her
15   ownership, too, was simply a question of money, of the price of the diamond ring on her left hand. This seems all too obvious; but it was the kind of truth which until that moment I'd only grasped theoretically.

The Aston-Martin started with a deep, healthy roar. As it passed
20   the cafe in the direction of St. Clair Road I noticed the young man's olive linen shirt and bright silk neckerchief. The collar of the shirt was tucked inside the jacket; he wore the rather theatrical ensemble with a matter-of-fact nonchalence. Everything about him was easy and loose but not tired or sloppy. He had an undistinguished face
25   with a narrow forehead and mousy hair cut short with no oil on it. It was a rich man's face, smooth with assurance and good living.

He hadn't ever had to work for anything he wanted; it had all been given him. The salary which I'd been so pleased about, an increase from Grade Ten to Grade Nine, would seem a pittance to
30   him. The suit in which I fancied myself so much – my best suit – would seem cheap and nasty to him. He wouldn't have a *best* suit; all his clothes would be the best.

For a moment I hated him. I saw myself, compared with him, as the Town Hall clerk, the subordinate pen-pusher, halfway to being
35   a zombie, and I tasted the sourness of envy. Then I rejected it . . . This didn't abate the fierceness of my longing. I wanted an Aston-Martin, I wanted a three-guinea linen shirt, I wanted a girl with a Riviera suntan – these were my rights, I felt, a signed and sealed legacy.

40   As I watched the tail-end of the Aston-Martin with its shiny new G.B. plate go out of sight I remembered the secondhand Austin Seven which the Efficient Zombie, Duffton's Chief Treasurer, had just treated himself to. That was the most the local government had to offer me; it wasn't enough. I made my choice then and there: I
45   was going to collect that legacy. It was as clear and compelling as the sense of vocation which doctors and missionaries are supposed to experience, though in my instance of course the call ordered me to do good to myself and not others.

Room at the Top, John Braine (1957)

Glossary
34   *subordinate pen-pusher* : someone of a low rank who does little more than copy things out
35   *zombie* : someone who automatically does a job without thinking
38   *Riviera sun-tan* : brown skin, obtained by sun-bathing in the south of France

4.4 Looking at vocabulary

Work in pairs to match the following words and phrases with the explanations below. Look back to where the words are used in the text to help you decide.

| grasped theoretically | pittance | envy | abate |
| treated himself | compelling | legacy | vocation |

- reduce
- bought for himself
- understood as an idea only
- money or property which is left to you when someone dies
- a job you do, not for the money, but for the love of it. Being a nurse, a teacher or a priest, perhaps
- _____ is wishing you had what someone else has got
- very small amount of money
- something which demands your attention is _____

4.5 Matching ideas with the text

Work in sets, A and B. Within the sets, work in pairs.
Match the following ideas with similar ideas in the text.

Set A

a) The young man had never had to earn any of the money he possessed.
b) I realised for the first time that it was only money which allowed this kind of man to possess an expensive car and a rich-looking girl.
c) When I compared my dull life with his, I really wished that I had what he had.

Set B

a) I decided at that moment that I was going to become rich.
b) One of my colleagues at the office had just bought a small used car. That was all he could get from our kind of job and it wasn't enough for me.
c) My pay would seem like nothing to him. My best clothes, which I thought I looked good in, would seem cheap to him.

Report to the class where in the text you have matched your ideas.

4.6 Discussion

Joe Lampton was a "material boy". He decided he was going to use all his energy to making himself rich. Have you ever seen something or somebody that has made you want to become rich? Compare examples.
Work in pairs to list all the ways you can think of to become rich. Compare your ideas with the class.

4.7 Class survey

Take a class vote about this statement.

> "It is better to have a job you like rather than one which is very well paid."

Now find out which of the texts in this section is most popular and which is most unpopular by taking a vote.

Theme 5 The World of Nature

Part 1

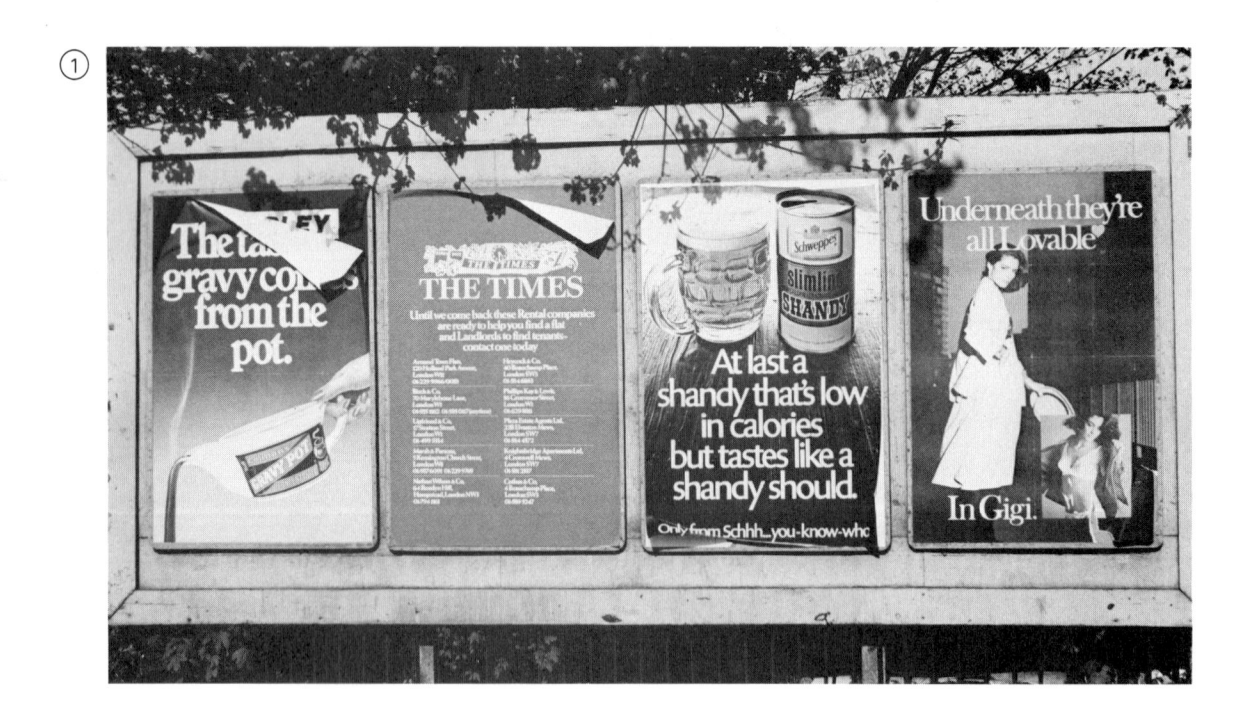

①

Text A Introductory Texts

> I think that I shall never see
> A poem lovely as a tree.
> Poems are made by fools like me
> But only God can make a tree.

(Alfred) Joyce Kilmer

> I think that I shall never see
> A billboard lovely as a tree.
> Indeed, unless the billboards fall
> I'll never see a tree at all.

Ogden Nash

Section four of this book, "The Root of all Evil", contained texts on the subject of money and wealth. For William Wordsworth, the experience of nature was a kind of wealth and many of his poems are about this subject. Text B, which is a poem by Wordsworth, is in fact one of the most famous poems in the English language.

1.1 Listening for general meaning

Listen to Text B and note down any words you hear that seem to be important. Compare your notes with the class and make a list on the board.

Text B I Wandered Lonely as a Cloud

> I wandered lonely as a cloud
> That floats on high o'er vales and hills,
> When all at once I saw a crowd,
> A host of golden daffodils;
> 5   Beside the lake, beneath the trees,
> Fluttering and dancing in the breeze.
>
> Continuous as the stars that shine
> And twinkle on the milky way,
> They stretched in never-ending line
> 10 Along the margin of the bay;
> Ten thousand saw I at a glance,
> Tossing their heads in sprightly dance.
>
> The waves beside them danced; but they
> Outdid the sparkling waves in glee;
> 15 A poet could not but be gay,
> In such a jocund company;
> I gazed – and gazed – but little thought
> What wealth the show had to me brought:

87 Talk About Literature

> For oft, when on my couch I lie
> 20 In vacant or in pensive mood,
> They flash upon that hidden eye
> Which is the bliss of solitude;
> And then my heart with pleasure fills,
> And dances with the daffodils.
>
> William Wordsworth (1804)
>
> **Glossary**
> 2   *vale* : small valley
> 8   *milky way* : the main group of stars in the solar system
> 22 *bliss* : great pleasure

1.2 Matching ideas with text

Work in two sets, A and B. Within the sets, work in pairs. Match the four short texts below with the four verses of the poem.
There are some difficult words in the poem. Note down which of these words are explained in the short texts.

Set A

a) Often when I'm sitting in my room relaxing or thinking, I remember the daffodils in my imagination. I become happy as I think of them dancing beside the lake.

b) There were as many of them as the stars shining in the night sky. There was an endless line of daffodils along the shore of the lake and in one glance I saw ten thousand of them dancing there.

Set B

c) The waves on the lake were dancing too but the daffodils were even more joyful than the waves. A poet could not help being cheerful looking at such a happy sight as this. I looked for a long time at the daffodils but never imagined what value I had got from them.

d) I was walking on my own one day when suddenly I saw a huge number of daffodils beside the lake and under the trees. They seemed to dance in the light wind that was blowing.

Report your ideas to the class.

1.3 Finding comparisons

Wordsworth compares the appearance of the daffodils with human behaviour. Work in pairs to find which words show this.
What else does Wordsworth compare the daffodils to?

1.4 Comparing prose with poetry

On the day that he saw the daffodils, Wordsworth's sister, Dorothy, was with him. Text C is what she wrote about the experience in her diary.
Read Text C but do not worry about words you do not understand. Work in two sets, A and B. Within the sets, work in pairs.

Set A should note down all the details which Wordsworth seems to have borrowed from his sister's diary description of the daffodils. Find any actual words that both of them use.

Set B should note down any ideas in the diary that Wordsworth did not use.

Report what you have found to the class. Make notes about what the other set tells you.

Text C   Thursday April 15th, 1802

It was a threatening misty morning but mild. We set off after dinner from Eusmere. Mrs Clarkson went a short way with us, but turned back. The wind was furious and we thought we must have returned. We first rested in the large boat-house, then under a furze
5 bush opposite Mr Clarkson's. We saw the plough going into the field. The wind seized our breath. The lake was rough. There was a boat by itself floating in the middle of the bay below Water Millock. We rested again in the Water Millock Lane. The hawthornes are black and green, the birches here and there
10 greenish, but there is yet more of purple to be seen on the twigs. We got over into a field to avoid some cows – people working. A few primroses by the roadside – woodsorrel flower, the anemone, scentless violets, strawberries, and that starry, yellow flower which Mrs C. calls pile wort. When we were in the woods beyond
15 Gowbarrow Park we saw a few daffodils close to the water-side. We fancied that the lake had floated the seeds ashore, and that the little colony had so sprung up. But as we went along there were more and more; and at last, under the boughs of the trees, we saw that there was a long belt of them along the shore, about the
20 breadth of a country turnpike road. I never saw daffodils so beautiful. They grew among the mossy stones about and about them; some rested their heads upon these stones as on a pillow for weariness; and the rest tossed and reeled and danced, and seemed as if they verily laughed with the wind, that blew upon them over
25 the lake; they looked so gay, ever glancing, ever changing. This wind blew directly over the lake to them. There was here and there a little knot, and a few stragglers a few yards higher up; but they were so few as not to disturb the simplicity, unity, and life of that one busy highway.

Dorothy Wordsworth

89 Talk About Literature

1.5 Making a more detailed comparison

Work in two sets, A and B. Within the sets, work in pairs.

Set A

Wordsworth used the word "breeze" to describe the light wind that was blowing over the lake. Note down any reference Dorothy makes to the **weather**.

Set B

Note down any words that you can guess are the names of **flowers, plants** or **trees**.

Report to the class what you have found.
What, then, are the main differences between the poem and the diary? What, in particular, has Wordsworth **changed** and **added**?
Which text do you prefer?

Part 2

2.1 Comparing a poem from the West with one from the East

You have looked at the differences between a poem and diary account of the same event. Now look at an example of one difference between Western and Eastern views of nature.

In pairs, first decide which picture matches Text D and which matches Text E. What seems to be the main difference between these two ways of approaching nature?

Text D

Flower in the crannied wall,
I pluck you out of the crannies,
I hold you here, root and all, in my hand,
Little flower – but if I could understand
What you are, root and all, and all in all,
I should know what God and man is.

Alfred Lord Tennyson (1869 – Nineteenth Century British)

Glossary
crannies : small cracks

Text E

Looking closely
There's a wild flower in bloom
Underneath the hedge

Basho (Seventeenth Century Japanese)

And rather than disturb the morning glory flower which was growing round his water bucket at the well, the Japanese poet Chiyo preferred to get his water from another place.

Text F

A morning glory
Twisted around my bucket –
I will ask my neighbour for water

Chiyo

2.2 Class survey

Take a class vote on which of these short poems is most popular.

2.3 Writing a short poem

To the Zen Buddhist, the simplest thing in nature can be the subject of a poem. Basho wrote many short poems about experiences in nature. These short poems are called haikus. One of his haikus is about a frog jumping into a pond.

Imagine yourself in the same situation as Basho. You are sitting in a garden, very quietly, and you see and hear a frog jumping into an old pond. Use no more than 12 words and, in pairs, try to write a poem about this experience. Use a dictionary if you need any new words.

2.4 Comparing poems

Now compare your poem with the following five translations of Basho's poem about the frog. Notice any similarities and any differences. Have you used the same words? Which of these five translations do you like the most?

Text G

a. It is an ancient pond
   A frog jumps in –
   The sound of water

b. The old pond
   A frog leaps in
   The sound of water

c. The still pond, ah!
   A frog leaps in:
   The water's sound.

d. Old pond
   jump-splash
   a frog

e. The old pond
   A frog jumps in
   Then a splash

Part 3

Text H returns to the idea of interfering with or disturbing nature. Its setting is at least a hundred years ago in the English countryside.
Jude Fawley's parents have died and he has gone to live with an old aunt. He doesn't like the part of the country where he now has to live and his only friend, the schoolmaster, has just left the village. Before he left, the schoolmaster gave Jude this advice: "Be a good boy, remember; and be kind to animals and birds, and read all you can."
Jude is now earning a very small amount of money scaring birds in the fields of one of the local farmers. He is using a "clacker", which is something to make a noise to keep the birds away from the seed in the fields.

3.1 Listening for general meaning

As you listen to the text, try to find out what problem Jude has with his job of scaring away the birds. Does the picture match the text well?

Text H

He sounded the clacker till his arm ached, and at length his heart grew sympathetic with the birds' thwarted desires. They seemed, like himself, to be living in a world which did not want them. Why should he frighten them away? They took upon them more and more the aspect of gentle friends – the only friends he could claim as being in the least degree interested in him, for his aunt had often told him that she was not. He ceased his rattling, and they alighted anew.

"Poor little dears!" said Jude aloud. "You *shall* have some dinner – you shall. There is enough for us all. Farmer Troutham can afford to let you have some. Eat, then, my dear little birdies, and make a good meal!"

They stayed and ate, inky spots on the nut-brown soil, and Jude enjoyed their appetite. A magic thread of fellow-feeling united his own life with theirs. Puny and sorry as those lives were, they much resembled his own.

His clacker he had by this time thrown away from him, as being a mean and sordid instrument, offensive both to the birds and himself as their friend. All at once he became conscious of a smart blow upon his buttocks, followed by a loud clack, which announced to his surprised senses that the clacker had been the instrument of offence used. The birds and Jude started up simultaneously, and the dazed eyes of the latter beheld the farmer in person, the great Troutham himself, his red face glaring down upon Jude's, the clacker swinging in his hand.

93 Talk About Literature

"So it's 'Eat, my dear birdies,' is it, young man? 'Eat, dear birdies,' indeed! I'll tickle your breeches, and see if you say, 'Eat, dear birdies,' again in a hurry! And you've been idling at the schoolmaster's too, instead of coming here, haven't you, eh? That's
30   how you earn your sixpence a day for keeping the rooks off my corn!"

Glossary
18   *sordid instrument* : unpleasant tool
21   *the clacker had been the instrument of offence used* : the clacker was what Farmer Troutham had used to hit Jude

3.2 Looking at vocabulary

Work in two sets, A and B. Within the sets, work in pairs. Match the words and phrases with the explanations below. Look back to the text to help you decide.

Set A

thwarted desires
tickle your breeches
alighted
resemble

Set B

puny
simultaneously
thread of fellow feeling
appetite

- eating with enjoyment
- landed on the ground
- things that they wanted to do but were prevented from doing
- be like or similar to something
- weak
- feeling sympathy
- beat you on the backside
- at the same time

If you don't know the meaning of any of the words and phrase in the other set's list, ask someone from that set to tell you.

Farmer Troutham beat Jude thoroughly with the clacker for not doing his job and sent him home. Jude was worried about what his aunt would say about him losing his job.

Text I

Though Farmer Troutham had just hurt him, he was a boy who could not himself bear to hurt anything. He had never brought home a nest of young birds without lying awake in misery half the

       night after, and often reinstating them and the nest in their original
  5   place the next morning. He could scarcely bear to see trees cut
       down or lopped from a fancy that it hurt them; and late pruning,
       when the sap was up and the tree bled profusely, had been a
       positive grief to him in his infancy.

Jude the Obscure, Thomas Hardy (1895)

   Glossary
3 *misery* : unhappiness
4 *reinstating* : putting back
6 *fancy* : belief
6 *late pruning* : cutting parts from trees in the spring instead of the autumn

3.3 Class survey

Was Jude stupid to think that trees can be hurt when they are cut or pruned? Take a class vote on whether you believe that plants can feel pain.

3.4 Comparing texts

Now read Text J to see if it agrees with your conclusion in 3.3. First check you know the meaning of the following words. Work in pairs and use a dictionary if necessary.

   reaction   shrimp   boiling   violent   ceremony   apologise

Text J

       In February 1966, an American called Cleve Backster made a
       fascinating discovery. He decided that he wanted to try to measure
       the rate at which water rose in a plant from the root to the leaf. In
       order to do this, he attached an instrument called a polygraph to
  5   each side of a leaf of a rubber plant he owned. The instrument is
       able to measure electrical resistance and is sometimes used to find
       out when human beings are telling lies.
       However, when he watered the rubber plant, his instrument
       showed no reaction. Backster decided to hurt the plant in some way
  10   to see if this produced any electrical reaction. First he dipped one of
       the leaves of the rubber plant into a cup of hot coffee and again
       there was no reaction. He then decided to burn the leaf of the plant
       with a match. At the very moment he made this decision, there was
       a sudden change in the instrument. It seemed that the plant had
  15   reacted to the idea that it was about to be burned. Backster was
       excited by this discovery and went on to test plants in other ways.
       He brought some live shrimps into his office and dropped them one
       by one into boiling water. Each time he did this the polygraph

recording jumped violently. When he dropped a dead shrimp into
20   the boiling water there was no reaction at all.
   Some of these findings suggest that plants do have feelings. For a long time certain tribes of North American Indians have used a ceremony whenever they chopped down trees. They believed that the trees felt pain when they did this and so they had ceremonies to
25   "apologise" to the tree before they began to chop it down. Perhaps such ceremonies are not as crazy as they seem.

3.5 Discussion

Work in pairs and make a list of the ways in which man changes or interferes with nature.

Discuss your ideas with the class and decide which of these ways **can** be avoided and which **cannot** be avoided.

3.6 Reading for general meaning

Work in two sets, A and B. Within the sets, work in pairs. Set A should read Text K and Set B should read Text L. Read very quickly and don't bother about detail. Just try to get a general idea of what the text is about. Decide also which of the pictures fits best with your text.

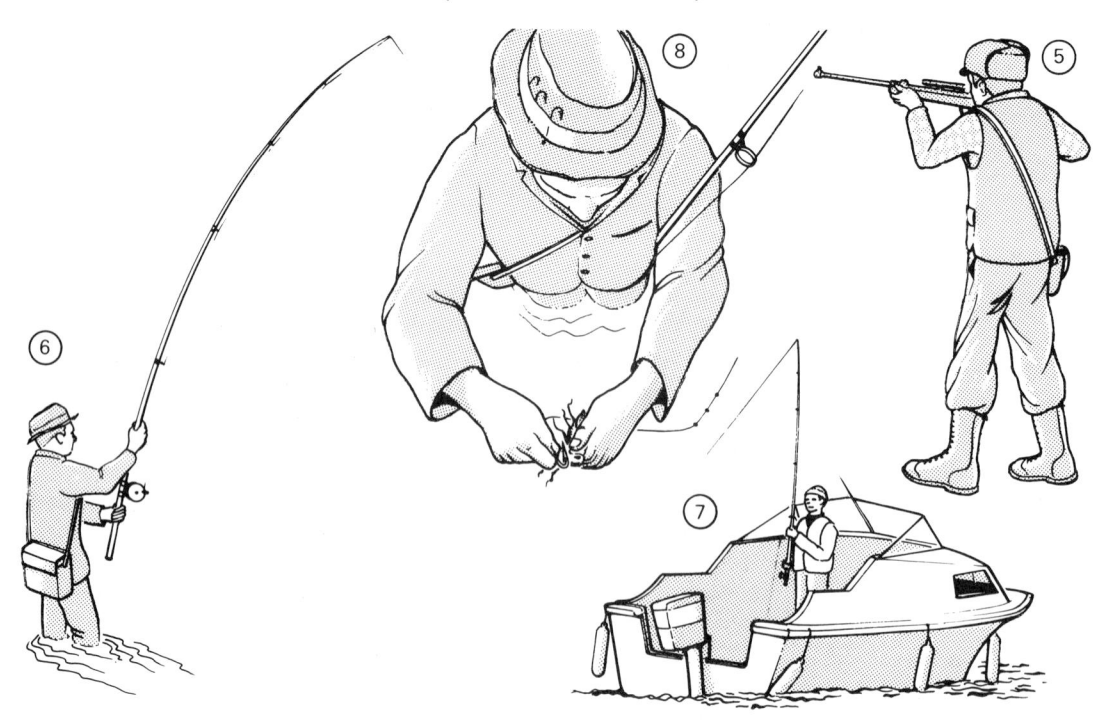

Tell the other set what your text is about and which picture matches it best.

Text K

He stepped into the stream. It was a shock. His trousers clung tight to his legs. His shoes felt the gravel. The water was a rising cold shock.
    Rushing, the current sucked against his legs. Where he stepped in, the water was over his knees. He waded with the current. The gravel slid under his shoes. He looked down at the swirl of water below each leg and tipped up the bottle to get a grasshopper.
    The first grasshopper gave a jump in the neck of the bottle and went out into the water. He was sucked under in the whirl by Nick's right leg and came to the surface a little way down the stream. He floated rapidly, kicking. In a quick circle, breaking the smooth surface of the water, he disappeared. A trout had taken him. Another hopper poked his head out of the bottle. His antennae wavered. He was getting his front legs out of the bottle to jump. Nick took him by the head and held him while he threaded the slim hook under his chin, down through his thorax and into the last segments of his abdomen. The grasshopper took hold of the hook with his front feet, spitting tobacco juice on it. Nick dropped him into the water.
    Holding the rod in his right hand he let out line against the pull of the grasshopper in the current. He stripped off line from the reel with his left hand and let it run free. He could see the hopper in the little waves of the current. It went out of sight.

Text L

There was a tug on the line. Nick pulled against the taut line. It was his first strike. Holding the now living rod across the current, he brought in the line with his left hand. The rod bent in jerks, the trout pumping against the current. Nick knew it was a small one. He lifted the rod straight up in the air. It bowed with the pull.
    He saw the trout in the water jerking with his head and body against the shifting tangent of the line in the stream.
    Nick took the line in his left hand and pulled the trout, thumping tiredly against the current, to the surface. His back was mottled the clear, water-over-gravel colour, his side flashing in the sun. The rod under his right arm, Nick stooped, dipping his right hand into the current. He held the trout, never still, with his moist right hand, while he unhooked the barb from his mouth, then dropped him back into the stream.
    He hung unsteadily in the current, then settled to the bottom beside a stone. Nick reached down his hand to touch him, his arm to the elbow under water. The trout was steady in the moving stream, resting on the gravel, beside a stone. As Nick's fingers

Talk About Literature

touched him, touched his smooth, cool, underwater feeling he was gone, gone in a shadow across the bottom of the stream.
He's all right, Nick thought. He was only tired.

From "Big Two-Hearted River", Ernest Hemingway (1930)

Glossary

- 2 *gravel* : small stones
- 7 *grasshopper* : a large, jumping insect, used here as bait to catch fish
- 9 *sucked under* : pulled under the water
- 12 *trout* : colourful fish, good for eating
- 16 *thorax* : chest
- 17 *abdomen* : lower body
- 18 *tobacco juice* : brown liquid from inside the insect
- 21 *current* : the flow of water in a river
- 24 *taut* : pulled tight
- 28 *bowed* : bent
- 36 *barb* : hook

3.7 Discussion

Now read the complete text more slowly. In pairs try to decide whether the character in the story is interfering with nature. If he **is** interfering, does this kind of interference matter? Discuss your ideas with the class.

Part 4

4.1 Discussion

The effects of nature are felt less in the town than in the country. Some people who live in towns or cities believe they have little or no contact with nature. Work in pairs and make a list of the ways nature can be seen in towns and cities.
Compare your ideas with the rest of the class.

4.2 Listening

Listen to the first nine lines of Text M and see if you can discover what its subject is? Then check your idea with the beginning of the text and the illustration on the next page.
How many people thought of this as an example of nature in a town?

4.3 Prediction

Have you ever seen snow falling in a city? If you have never seen snow at all, try to imagine what it would be like.
The lines you just listened to come from a poem by Robert Bridges, called "London Snow". What do you think he described in this poem? What sights and sounds and events?
What words and phrases do you associate with snow?
Compare your ideas with the rest of the class and list them on the board.

4.4 Looking at vocabulary

Before you read the poem, find out the meaning of the words below. Note down the ideas you expect to be linked to these words.
For example, the word "veiling" is used in the poem. "Veil" is usually linked with a wedding, since it is the covering a bride sometimes wears over her face. There is nothing about weddings in the poem. Why then is "veiling" used?
Work in two sets, A and B. Within the sets, work in pairs.

Set A

stealthily
drowsy
sailing
train

Set B

hushing
drifting
lazily
moss

Ask members of the other set if you do not know the meaning of words in their list. Compare the ideas you linked with these words.

4.5 Reading and listening

Now read the poem while you listen to it.
How many of the ideas you listed on the board for 4.3 can you find in the poem?

Text M London Snow

    When men were all asleep the snow came flying,
    In large white flakes on the city brown,
    Stealthily and perpetually settling and loosely lying,
    Hushing the latest traffic of the drowsy town;
5   Deadening, muffling, stifling its murmurs failing;
    Lazily and incessantly floating down and down:
    Silently sifting and veiling road, roof and railing;
    Hiding differences, making unevenness even,
    Into angles and crevices softly drifting and sailing.
10 All night it fell, and when full inches seven
    It lay in the depth of its uncompacted lightness,
    The clouds blew off from a high and frosty heaven;
    And all woke earlier for the unaccustomed brightness
    Of the winter dawning, the strange unheavenly glare:
15 The eye marvelled – marvelled at the dazzling whiteness;
    The ear hearkened to the stillness of the solemn air;
    No sound of wheel rumbling nor of foot falling,
    And the busy morning cries came thin and spare.
    Then boys I heard, as they went to school, calling,
20 They gathered up the crystal manna to freeze
    Their tongues with tasting, their hands with snowballing;
    Or rioted in a drift, plunging up to the knees;
    Or peering up from under the white-mossed wonder,
    "O look at the trees!" they cried, "O look at the trees!"
25 With lessened load a few carts creak and blunder,
    Following along the white deserted way,
    A country company long dispersed asunder:
    When now already the sun, in pale display
    Standing by Paul's high dome, spread forth below
30 His sparkling beams, and awoke the stir of day.
    For now doors open, and war is waged with the snow;
    And trains of sombre men, past tale of number,
    Tread long brown paths, as toward their toil they go:
    But even for them awhile no care encumber
35 Their mind diverted; the daily word is unspoken,
    The daily thoughts of labour and sorrow slumber
    At the sight of the beauty that greets them, for the charm
       they have broken

Robert Bridges (c1890)

Glossary

3	*perpetually*	: all the time
5	*muffling, stifling*	: making silent
9	*crevices*	: small gaps between stones and bricks
11	*uncompacted*	: not pressed down, lying loose
14	*glare*	: brightness
20	*manna*	: food
22	*rioted in a drift*	: fighting in deep snow
25	*blunder*	: move awkwardly, in wrong directions
27	*a country company long dispersed asunder*	: people from the countryside spreading out through the city
29	*Paul's high dome*	: St. Paul's Cathedral, a large London church
30	*stir*	: movement
32	*sombre*	: gloomy or dismal, unhappy-looking
34	*care encumber*	: worries weighing them down, making them sad
37	*charm*	: magic effect

4.6 Deciding on the mood of a text

In pairs try to decide which **two** of the following words best expresses the mood of Text M?

amazement   anger   confusion   sadness   worry   humour

Try to find the place in the poem where the mood changes.

4.7 Examining the use of sounds and verb forms

Work in two sets, A and B. Within the sets, work in pairs to look carefully at the **sounds** in the first 12 lines of the poem.

Set A

Make a list of all the words containing 'l' sounds.

Set B

Make a list of all the words containing 's' sounds.

Report to the class what you have found.
Then work in pairs to make a list of all '-ing' verbs you can find in the first 25 lines.

4.8 Discussion

Do you think there is any reason for repeating sounds and verb forms? Do you enjoy the effect they create?
Now search the poem quickly to see if you can find other examples of sounds being repeated or '-ing' verbs being used a lot.
Do you like Bridge's picture of snow in the city? Does it have the right feeling and can you see the pictures clearly?

4.9 Explaining ideas

Bridges says that the men going to work at the end of the poem are waging war against the snow. They have also broken the charm or spoiled the magic effect of the morning. How have they done this?

Now look at a schoolgirl's description of the same magic being broken.

Text N Snow

> In the country
> Still and silent
> As smooth as velvet
> With a strong taste of peppermint
> 5 Undisturbed.
> While in towns
> Its silent sleep is broken
> By industry and human pleasure
> And it lies
> 10 Muddy slushy beaten
> And dead

Juliet George (Aged 12) (1987)

4.10 Looking at contrasting adjectives

The effect of this short poem can be seen by looking at the adjectives used. In pairs, note down the adjectives describing the country snow and the town snow. Look up any you don't know the meaning of.
Which do you think is the most powerful adjective? Why?

4.11 Comparing poems

Work in two sets, A and B. Within the sets, work in pairs.

Set A should note down all the **similarities** between Text M and Text N.

Set B should note down all the **differences** between Text M and Text N.

Report to the class what you have found and complete a list of similarities and differences as you hear what others have to say.
Which poem do you like best? Do you know why?

4.12 Matching ideas with poems

Poems, as we have seen, can be even shorter than Text N. Before leaving the subject of snow, read the four haikus below and find out the meaning of any words you don't know. Use a dictionary if necessary.
The haikus have a similar theme but they express different ideas.
Two of them contain contrasts of colour, **one** of them expresses great enjoyment of the snow and **one** looks forward to the season which comes after winter.
Work in pairs to identify which of the haikus expresses the ideas just mentioned. Can you find any of the same ideas in Texts M and N?

Text O

Snow-swallowed valley:
Only the river painted
A black, winding line

        Boncho

Text P

Even as the snow fell
Through it came whispering
A breath of Spring

        Basho

Text Q

Snowy morning –
One crow passing
After another

        Basho

Text R

Come, let's go
Snow-viewing
Until it buries us

        Basho

4.13 Discussion

Nature in towns seems to be controlled. But nature can never really be controlled although man has always tried to do so. Work in pairs and make a list of examples of problems and difficulties which nature can cause. Make a list on the blackboard.
Have you experienced any of these natural difficulties in your own life? Which of these aspects of nature **can** be controlled?
One text in the first section of this book, "The Golden Gates of Childhood", is about a problem caused by nature. Look through that section very quickly and see if you can find it. What is the problem described there?

103   Talk About Literature

Part 5

Text S/T is by James Nguji, a writer from East Africa. His story is about one aspect of nature which **cannot** be controlled. The main character is an African called Joshua, who is a Christian priest.

5.1   Looking at vocabulary

First work in two sets, A and B. Within the sets, work in pairs. Check you know the meaning of the following words.

Set A

rivalry
convert
threaten
affect
pray

Set B

sacrifice
persuade
missionary
victory
comfort

5.2   Finding specific information

Read Text S. Work in two sets, A and B. Within the sets, work in pairs. Look for the following information.

Set A

Decide which of the buildings shown here best depicts where Joshua, the village priest, lives. Why do you think this house is "the only one of its kind along the ridge"?

Set B

Find the word in the text which means a great shortage of water. Note down the effects of the water shortage which are mentioned.

⑩ ⑪ ⑫

Report to the class what you have found.

Text S

Joshua, the village priest, watched the gathering black clouds and muttered one word – 'Rain'. It was almost a whisper, spoken so quietly that a man a yard away would not have heard it. He was standing on a raised piece of ground looking thoughtfully at the clouds and the country around. Behind him stood a tin-roofed rectangular building from which thick black smoke was beginning to issue, showing that the woman of the house had already come from the shamba and was now preparing the evening meal. This was his house – the only one of its kind along the ridge, and beyond. The rest were mud-walled, grass-thatched round huts that were scattered all over the place. From these also black smoke was beginning to curl upwards.

Joshua knew that in most of the huts the inmates had been sleeping with contracting, wrinkled stomachs, having eaten nothing or very little. He had seen such cases in the past months during his rounds of comforting the hungry and the suffering, promising them that God would in time bring rain. For the drought had been serious, and had lasted many months, so that crops in the field had sickened, while some had dried up altogether. Cows and goats were so thin that they could hardly give enough milk.

If it rained now it would be a blessing for everyone, and perhaps crops would revive and grow and all would be well. The dry anxious looks of the faces of mothers and fathers would disappear. Again he looked at the darkening clouds and slowly the old man retraced his steps to the house.

Soon it began to rain! Menacing thunderstorms boomed in the heavens and the white spots of lightning flashed across with a sharpness and fury that frightened him. Standing near a window, the priest, his horse-shoe-shaped bald head lined with short grey bristles of hair, watched the slanting raindrops striking the hard ground and wetting it. 'Jehovah! He has won!' the priest muttered breathlessly. He felt cheated, bitter and angry.

Glossary
9 *ridge* : a section of high ground
10 *grass-thatched* : roofs made with cut grass
14 *contracting* : getting smaller
18 *crops* : plants grown for food

5.3 Discussion and prediction

Can you imagine why Joshua feels cheated, bitter and angry that the rain has begun? Who do you think Joshua is talking about when he says, "He has won!"? Read Text T to find out.

Text T

For he knew that the coming of rain so soon after the morning sacrifice would be nothing but a victory for the rain-maker at whose request a black ram had been sacrificed. Yes. This was the culmination of their long fight, their long struggle and rivalry in Makuyu village.

Makuyu was an isolated little place. Even the nearest missionary station was some fifty-five miles off – quite a long way in a country without roads. It was in fact one of the last areas to be seriously affected by the coming of the white missionaries, farmers and administrators. And so while the rest of the country had already seen the rain-maker, the witch-doctor and black-magic workers being challenged by Christianity, this place had remained pretty well under the power and guidance of the rainmaker.

The challenge and rivalry here began when the Rev. Livingstone of Thabaini Mission made a visit and initiated Joshua into this new mystery – the new religion. The white man's God, creator of everything. And the rain-maker (he was also a magic-worker) had denounced his rivals when he saw how many people had been converted by Joshua into this new faith. He had felt angry and tried to persuade people not to follow Joshua. He threatened them with plague and death. But nothing had happened. The rain-maker had even threatened Joshua.

But Joshua had not minded. Why should he? Had he not received an assurance from Livingstone that this new God would be with him 'always, even unto the end of the earth'?

Then the drought had come. And all the time Joshua told the village that there would be rain. And all the time he prayed over and over again for it to come down. Nothing had happened. The rain-maker said the drought was the anger of the old God. He, the rain-maker, was the only person who could intercede for the people. Today, under the old sacred tree – Mugamo – a black ram, without any blemish, was sacrificed. Now it had rained! All that morning Joshua had prayed, asking God not to send rain on that particular day. Please God, my God, do not bring rain today. Please God, my God, let me defeat the rain-maker and your name shall be glorified. But in spite of his entreaties it had rained.

From "The Village Priest", James Ngugi (1965)

Glossary

34 *rain-maker* : somebody who seemed to have skill at causing rain to fall by using magic
36 *culmination* : end point or climax
44 *challenged by* : questioned or attacked
47 *initiated* : introduced
50 *denounced his rivals* : said bad things about those who were competing with him, those who had accepted the Christian religion
59 *prayed* : talked to God, and in this case asked for something
62 *intercede* : ask someone (in this case God) to do something for someone else
67 *your name shall be glorified* : you will be admired and perhaps worshipped

5.4 Guessing the meaning of words

There are a number of unusual words in Text S/T but many of them can be guessed by looking closely at the sentences where they are found. Don't worry about the **exact** meaning but work in pairs to try to guess the **general** meaning of these words.

inmates – these are sleeping in the huts
sickened – what would happen to the crops in a drought?
blessing – how would people feel if it did begin to rain?
revive – what would happen to the crops if the rain came?
lightning – what flashes during a thunderstorm?
challenged by – what might Christianity do to the rain-maker and the black-magic workers?
plague – the rain-maker threatens those who follow Joshua with death. What else could he threaten them with?
entreaties – what had Joshua done to try to stop the rain?

5.5 Looking at descriptive language

James Ngugi did not spend much time describing the coming of rain in detail. In pairs, note down what words he used to describe the change of the weather.

5.6 Listening for the main subject

Text U is a poem by a writer from the same part of Africa as James Ngugi. Listen to the poem and try to notice anything which links it with Text S/T.

Text U

     From the west
     Clouds come hurrying with the wind
     – turning
     – sharply turning
5   Here and there
     Like a plague of locusts
     – whirling
     Tossing things up on its tail
     – hurrying
10 Like a madman chasing nothing

     Pregnant
     They gather to perch on hills
     Like dark sinister wings,
     The wind whistles furiously by
15 And trees bend to let it pass.

     In the villages
     Screams of delighted children
     Toss and turn
     In the din of whirling wind,
20 – women
     Babies clinging on their backs
     – dart about
     – in and out
     – madly

25 Clothes
     Wave like tattered flags
     Flying off
     To expose dangling breasts
     As jaggered blinding flashes
30 rumble
     tremble
     and crack!
     Amidst the smell of fired smoke
     In the rumbling belly of the storm.

                              David Rubadiri (1965)

Glossary
6   *locusts* : insects which eat a lot of leaves and so destroy crops
29 *jaggered* : jagged, the broken line of lightning
34 *belly* : stomach

5.7 Deciding on a title

Work in pairs to think of a suitable title for this poem.

Which of these titles do you think is the one which David Rubadiri chose?

The End of the Drought   Birds in the Storm
An African Thunderstorm   A Windy Day

5.8 Comparing the language of two texts

Work in two sets, A and B. Within the sets, work in pairs. Look for the following language details.

Set A

Look back at Text M, "London Snow". Compare the **verb forms** with those in Text U. Can you see any similarities?
Then list all the verbs of **movement** in the Rubadiri poem.

Set B

Look back at Text M, "London Snow". Look at the **end words** of the lines and see if there are any words which rhyme. Is there a pattern of rhymes? Are there any rhymes in the Rubadiri poem?
Then list all the **sounds** you can find in the Rubadiri poem.

Report to the class what you have discovered.

5.9 Looking at comparisons

David Rubadiri makes several comparisons in his poem. Work in pairs to look at these comparisons. Try to find what the **wind**, the **clouds** and the **clothes** are compared to.
Do you think these comparisons work well?

5.10 Discussion

Is Rubadiri's poem effective? How does he create his picture of the storm?

5.11 Review and Discussion

Look back over the texts you have read from this section. How many of them describe experiences you have had? Make a list. Are these the texts you like best?

Tapescripts

Tapescript 1

S1: My first impression... I think this poem is about the happiness of a schoolboy – look at the way it begins: "I love to rise...". He's happy at the beginning of the day when he gets up. The sun seems to be shining... and he talks about the "sweet company"...

S2: But what does he mean by "sweet company"?

S1: Well, he means his friends, the friends he goes to school with, doesn't he?

T: No, that's not right. The friends are the skylark and the huntsman... he hears these when he gets up, perhaps out of the window of his bedroom.

S1: OK... so he lives in the country, right? And he's very happy... the poem is about his happiness... that's what I said first of all...

T: Yes, alright, he's happy... but look at the second verse. That's not so happy. The poet says "it drives all joy away"... sounds very negative. Tell me, *what* drives all joy away?

S2: Well, it's school... it's going to school on a morning in summer, that's what it says...

S1: Right. I see that. He's unhappy about going to school. Well, that's normal, isn't it? Who likes going to school? It's like a prison for lots of people.

S2: Well, I like going to school, actually... we do some really interesting things... at least sometimes. It's not a prison to me...

T: I'm glad *you* don't think school is a prison, but what about in the poem? Is there anything about prison there?

S1: No, I don't think there is...

S2: But look at the fourth verse... What's that about, "How can a bird sit in a cage"?

T: Good. That's a prison, isn't it? A cage is a prison for a bird...

S1: Mmm... I see. So the bird is the schoolboy.

T: Well, the bird in the cage is *like* the schoolboy... Look at this..."How can a child, when fears annoy, But droop his tender wing." That's the child being like a bird again. Because children don't have wings, do they? It means, what else can a child do when he is afraid, what else can he do but droop... hang down his head.

S2: Yes, that's good, I like that... but the next bit is hard, something about buds and blossoms...

S1: Yes, it's about trees and plants... I can't understand it. Summer fruit? What's that about?

T: Well, suppose the child is like a bud on a plant, which is damaged when it is very young... think about that possibility...

Tapescript 2

T: Well, we know what the toad means in this poem, don't we? Larkin already wrote about that in his poem "Toads". Now, this is called "Toads Revisited". What do you think that means?

S1: I think it probably means that he's writing about work again...

T: Yes, I should think so... now did he like work in that first poem?

S2: No, he didn't. He thought that work stopped him from being free...

T: Right. Well, let's look at what he's saying here. What's the first part of the poem about? What does he say at the beginning?

S2: He describes being in a park...

T: Yes...

S1: And he says it should feel better than work being there.

T: Right... that's interesting. He's free, out in a park, in the sunshine and he says it *should* feel better than work. Why does he say *should*?

S2: Because it *doesn't* feel better than work... I don't know why.

T: Right. He seems to say that it *isn't* better than work, being out in the park... in fact he says "it doesn't suit me". Well, what sort of work does he do? Perhaps it's very interesting work... can we tell that from the poem?

S1: It's not very interesting work. He seems to work in an office... he talks about his secretary...

T: Anything else?

S2: Yes, something about keeping a call in... the secretary says, "Shall I keep the call in Sir..."

T: Good. His secretary is answering the telephone and wants to know if she should keep the call connected... it's office work of some kind. There's an in-tray mentioned, too. That's a box for putting papers...

S1: OK. So he works in an office and that's not very interesting... so why doesn't he like being out in the park, why doesn't it suit him?

T: Well, lets look at what is happening in the park. He sees all sorts of people there, doesn't he? Now what are those people doing? Look at verse 5... he says they're all dodging the toad work... escaping from it... but then he says "Think of being them!" You say that when you would *like* to be someone else or perhaps when you *don't want* to be someone else... now, tell me what those people are doing...

S2: They're hearing the clock strike the hours, they're watching bread being delivered... that's in verse 6...

S1: And watching the children going home and the sun going behind the clouds...

T: Right. And they're also thinking about their failures, aren't they?... Now, do these things sound very interesting or exciting?

S1: No, they don't. And that's why he'd rather be in his office, with a job... he doesn't want to be unemployed.

T: Yes, that's it. He's happy to have his job, even if it's not very interesting... so what do you think that last verse means: "Give me your arm, old toad; Help me down Cemetery Road"? Why Cemetery Road?

S2: Well, a cemetery is where people are buried, so the road he's walking on goes beside a cemetery.

T: Maybe... but it probably means a bit more... perhaps it means that he's going to keep working until he dies... work will help him on the way to the end of his life...

Key

The Golden Gates of Childhood

1.1 Discussion (p.3)

Set A
The picture matches Text c.
Texts a, b, e and g.

Set B
Text d is intended to be humorous.
Texts c and f talk about children's behaviour.

1.3 Deciding the mood of a text (p.3)

The first verse seems happy and positive – "happy", "merry", "welcome", "sing", "cheerful".

1.4 Looking at language and meaning (p.4)

Set A
Sounds: bells, birds singing, echoes of children playing. The two voices are the children (9) and the old folk (16).

Set B
Youth and age, early morning (1) and evening (23). The end of the day might express the passing of childhood.

2.2 Deciding on the mood of a text (p.5)

Fear

2.4 Finding out how mood is created (p.6)

Set A
The fowls, particularly the cock, geese, dark store room, story of Lazarus.

Set B
menacing, ferocious, shiver, waddling after me, fierce, frightened.

2.5 Looking at verb forms (p.7)

The past form is much more common in telling stories. The only example of past form is "Lazarus was raised", this being part of Peggotty's story. Dickens uses the present form to make the reader feel that David Copperfield is remembering things now. The memories thus seem more striking, more immediate, and the present form shows how clear they are to David.

3.2 Looking at vocabulary (p.8)

Order of definitions: wire, selfish, plumber, icicle, frost, choke.

3.4 Finding out how mood is created (p.9)

A good break point is line 24 with "Selfish little pig".

Set A
Positive: "wonderful" (twice), "marvelled", "happier" (twice), "Christmas", "birthday". There are no negative ideas.

Set B
Negative: "selfish" (3 times), "poor" (3 times), many repetitions of "not", "no", "nor" – "no nice porridge", "couldn't love", "no fun". Also "choked" and "bitter knowledge". There are no positive ideas.

The nurse is rather rough, insensitive and unkind.

3.5 Comparing rhyme schemes (p.10)

The rhyme scheme of Text B is AABBCCDDEE. There is no rhyme scheme in Text D although some words are repeated at the end of lines: "wonderful", "garden", "icicles" and "heart".

3.9 Examining the use of sound words (p.12)

Set A
shrieked, demonaical noise, shrieking, thuds, booming shouts, sharp replies, bang, snarling shout, man's voice got higher

Set B
piercing medley of shrieks, cries, silent, lull, hummed, whistled, shrieked, silence (3 times), tramp, drumming

3.10 Looking at an aspect of mood (p.12)

Set A
Positive words: liked, peace, morning, happy (3 times)

Set B
Negative words: hated, very bad, night, vastness, terror (twice), anguish (twice), conflicts, drunk, nasty, suspense, horror (twice), blood (twice), darkness, anxiety

3.11 Discussion (p.13)

"Night" is linked with all the negative words and "morning" with positive words. Night therefore expresses the suffering of the children and morning is associated with relief from their suffering.

4.5 Looking at the structure of the story (p.17)

Present: lines 1-20, 58-65. Past: lines 21-57.

4.6 Identifying the sense of touch (p.17)

Set A
buttocks to fit boards, hands and feet to touch steel, fragments fell on his face, thrill travelled his body, indentation in the grass, hand pressing on his shoulder.

Set B
pain biting into his shoulder, bundle pressed deeper, pain across his shoulders

The two different kinds of feelings are those of enjoyment and those of pain.

4.7 Indentifying change of mood (p.17)

Change occurs at line 33, when the attendant interrupts. "Freedom", "joy" and "happiness" might be the mood before the change and "confusion", "anger" or "pain" afterwards.

Text D, "Plumbers", is very similar to Text G/H, with its sudden change of mood in the middle.

4.8 Searching for words (p.18)

Set A
chute (sometimes called "slide"), swings, merry-go-round (sometimes called "roundabout"), see-saw. fragments, particles.

Set B
children, attendant, coloureds, whites, mothers, babies, nurse girls.
The white boy is called "a detached spectator" (that is, no longer involved).

4.9 Discussion (p.18)

The swing represents freedom, happiness and the world of childhood while the bundle of clothes represents repression, loss of freedom and the adult world. The swing in Text F probably has much the same meaning of freedom and happiness, although there is no sense of repression in that text.

5.5 Deciding on the mood of a text (p.21)

Sadness

5.6 Comparing texts (p.22)

"Puff" is about a child beginning to grow up and leave his toys behind. The nearest to this idea is the extract from Peter Pan (g), where Peter says he doesn't want to grow up.

The Happiest Days of Your Life

1.1 Deciding about attitudes (p.23)

Positive: d. The rest are negative.

1.5 Matching pictures with text (p.26)

Illustration 2 best matches the strict kind of teacher described.

1.6 Matching descriptions (p.27)

Gradgrind is a man who likes to calculate everything carefully. Words and phrases: facts, realities, ruler and pair of scales, weigh and measure, question of figures.

1.10 Giving a title (p.31)

Dickens' title was "Murdering the Innocents".

1.11 Matching diagram to text (p.31)

Diagram 3, which represents a very dominant teacher, best describes the teacher/student relationship in the Dickens text.

1.12 Word sorting and discussion (p.32)

1. art, doubt, freedom, imagination, creative.
2. fact, mechanical, certainty, science, control.
List 2 links with the text.

2.3 Listening to a discussion (p.33)

Set A
In his bedroom
The season of summer
In the classroom

Set B
A caged bird
The teacher
Growing buds on a tree

2.4 Supporting an opinion (p.34)

Positive: love, sweet, joy (3 times), youthful spring, summer, summer fruit, bless, mellowing.
Negative: cruel, outworn, sighing, dismay, drooping, anxious, nor (twice), dreary shower, fears annoy, droop, buds are nipped, blossoms blown away, plants are stripped, sorrow and care's dismay, griefs.

Negative ideas, being much more frequent, express the overall mood of the poem, which is negative towards being restricted by school.

2.8 Checking and discussion (p.35)

Paxton's song is about propaganda and "thought

113 Talk About Literature

control" in school. The boy in the song believes everything he has been told and then repeats it. The song is therefore similar to the idea in *The Wall*. Blake does not refer directly to thought control in school, but he is concerned about restrictions which do not allow a child to grow up in a natural way.

3.1 Looking at vocabulary (p.36)

Order of definitions: panic, handle, deceitful, distaste, encounter, junk, get away with, inspect.

3.3 Matching pictures with text (p.38)

Illustration 6: 46-48. Illustration 7: 61-62. Illustration 8: 15-21.

3.3 Matching sentences with text (p.39)

Set A 46-48, 3-4
Set B 31-33, 8-10

3.5 Retelling the story (p.39)

The main points are: the headmaster talks to the smokers about their crime, he asks them to empty their pockets and finds nothing, the smokers threaten the messenger with looks, the headmaster discovers the cigarettes on the messenger, they are all punished, but the messenger suffers most because he doesn't know how to hold his hand in order to protect it.

3.6 Comparing texts (p.39)

Text I/J in "The Golden Gates" is most similar to Text H in this section. In both cases someone is blamed for something they did not do and the blame was put onto them by other children.

4.3 Looking at the language of description (p.42)

A writer living in the country would probably compare things with nature and with animals.

Set A
Hopkins is compared to a bullock, that is a very large and solid young animal. Words: heavy, full-grown, thick-legged, red-fisted, bursting with flesh, designed for the great outdoors, physically out of scale (that is, too big for the schoolroom).

Set B
Crabby B is compared to a yellow cat. Words: sour (at her sourest), awful leer, spitting and clawing with rage.

4.4 Comparing texts (p.42)

Similarities: behaviour problems, teachers trying to control students.
Differences: Text H shows a large school, Text I/J a small one. The headmaster remains calm while the headmistress loses her temper and gets very angry.

The boys in Text H have been caught smoking but it seems that the headmistress in Text I/J is angry with Hopkins for no good reason. The headmaster actually punishes the boys while the headmistress does nothing to punish Hopkins. The boys in Text H submit to the headmaster while Hopkins rebels against his teacher.

4.6 Listening for the main idea (p.42)

The main voice in the poem is that of a teacher. The girl refuses to write an essay on what she considers to be a stupid title.

4.7 Comparing texts (p.44)

Lines 18-19, "place myself in a position to tower over her" correspond with diagram 3, which shows the teacher very dominant over the student.

4.9 Review and survey (p.44)

"The Essay" is about rebellion in class and for that reason it is very similar to Text I/J. The dominant, self-confident teacher is also similar to Gradgrind in Texts B-E and perhaps Crabby B in Text I/J.

All Work and No Play

1.2 Deciding about attitudes (p.46)

Work is a good idea: b, e. Not so good: a, c, d, f

1.5 Matching pictures with text (p.48)

Illustration 2 matches Text B, Illustration 3 Text C, Illustration 4 Text I, Illustration 5 Text E, Illustration 6 Text D.

1.6 Listening for general meaning (p.48)

Probably Introductory Text c is nearest in feeling to Text B – idleness.

2.1 Looking at vocabulary (p.49)

Order of explanations: accuracy, unconsciousness, hell, exhausting, pursuit, automatic, consolation, experiment, sever

2.2 Making a summary (p.50)

Set A
Text C describes all the writing and studying Martin does. It tells how happy he is with all this work and how he does not have enough time to do everything he wants. He finds it difficult to stop doing one thing in order to begin the next and dislikes having to waste time on sleep.

Set B
Text D describes in detail Martin's exhausting and automatic labour in the laundry. Here the work is so physically tiring that he has no time or energy to think.

He hates this work because he feels that his employer has taken over his mind as well as his body.

2.3 Finding specific information (p.50)

Set A
Phrases only of liking: profoundly happy, extremely exciting, joy of creation, days were too short, joyfully, regret that he ceased from writing, hated ceasing to live, glorious day.

Set B
Activities: writing articles, writing short stories, reading (go to the reading room), borrowing books from the library, studying the algebra of physics, seeing Ruth, sleeping.

2.4 Looking at language and vocabulary (p.51)

Set A
broke his stride, broke off, ceased from, tore himself away from, stand up and go, shut up (the book), put the notebook and pencil aside, ceasing to live.

Set B
a) tore himself away from that chart room of knowledge, b) the jangling bell would jerk him out of unconsciousness, c) he scorched through the dark streets, d) it was like severing heart-strings to stand up and go.

2.6 Reading and noting (p.52)

Unpleasant, air was sizzling, stove roared red hot, irons sent up clouds of steam, sweat poured from Martin, heat of the day, exertions, nerve-wracking, body-destroying toil, driven soul, crawled into bed, hell.

3.2 Listening (p.54)

Arthur Seaton's favourite day is Friday. He likes it because he is paid on that day. He works in a factory.

3.3 Guessing meanings (p.55)

"fogged up" is when you find it difficult to focus or to see.
"excruciating din" means terrible noise.
"the gaffer" means the boss.

3.4 Identifying words that are not important (p.55)

Set A
Working of machines: cutting, drilling, boring, rough-threading, flying and flapping belts.

Set B
Machine parts: steel cylinders, motor-trolleys, belts, motor, stops, jigs, lathe.

3.5 Discussion: comparing types of work (p.56)

Martin could not continue partly because the work was so physically hard. But more important was the fact that he could no longer think. Arthur is able to continue because he forgets about the actual work and finds it easy to amuse himself by thinking about his leisure time.

4.4 Searching for a word (p.59)

The word not used in the text is "luxury" but the examples of luxuries are: rich carpets, fine furniture, delicate cookery, big house.

4.6 Finding the general meaning (p.60)

Larkin says he likes, or perhaps more accurately, accepts work.

4.7 Matching pictures with text (p.61)

The hare-eyed clerk with the jitters (12) is not illustrated.

The Root of All Evil

1.1 Deciding about attitudes (p.65)

Positive: c, d, f. Negative: a, b, e, g

1.2 Discussion (p.66)

In Text b at the beginning of "The Golden Gates", Lewis Carroll says that he would give all the money that life has brought him to be a little child again for one day.

2.1 Looking at vocabulary (p.69)

Order of explanations: passion, wander, conscious, accumulate, solitary, satisfaction, monotony, imprisonment.

2.2 Collecting key words (p.70)

The most important words would probably be: guineas, money, passion, counted.

2.3 Finding ideas in the text (p.72)

Set A
"He began to think the money was conscious of him" (9-10). The coins had "faces" (12). "he took them out to enjoy their companionship" (15). He thought of the guineas to be earned in the future "as if they had been unborn children" (35).

Set B
Silas' life is compared to a river (43-45) which has become only a small trickle of water, cutting a narrow way through unfertile ground.
The picture matches lines 12-13.

115 Talk About Literature

2.4 Finding out how word pictures are created (p.72)

The picture of Silas as a miser: wanted the heaps to grow (7), He handled them, he counted them (12-13), their form and colour were like the satisfaction of a thirst (13-14), his revelry (25), closed his shutters (26), made fast his doors, and drew out his gold (26), heap of coins (27), thick leather bags (28), How the guineas shone (29), He spread them out in heaps and bathed his hands in them, counted them, felt their rounded outline (30-33).

2.8 Deciding on the mood of a text (p.75)

Humour.

2.9 Comparing texts (p.75)

Set A
The texts are both about robberies and are therefore both about greed. When the robber arrives the house in each case is empty and so the robber is able to take his chance.

Set B
In Texts C-E, a man with a lot of money is being robbed; in Text F, the monk has nothing. The monk returns while the robber is there; Silas does not. Silas wants to keep his property; the monk does not mind losing it. Texts C-E are entirely serious while Text F is humorous.

3.4 Looking at vocabulary (p.78)

The three words are used to emphasize the strange mental and physical state that Nyagar was in. He was very unsure what to do, his mind was empty and his body could hardly move. These words relate to the other aspects of Nyagar's condition examined in the next task.

3.5 Finding out how a person is described (p.78)

Set A
changed his mind (2), Did I close the gate? (8), Was somebody coming? (18) (both show nervousness and uncertainty).

Set B
nervously (21), he thought his heart had stopped (24), just nervous (26), echo of his footsteps bothered him (26-27), undecided (30), felt nervous (32).

4.1 Reading and finding words (p.80)

Money words: credit, cash, material, pay, interest, pennies, rich

4.4 Looking at vocabulary (p.83)

Order of explanations: abate, treated himself, grasped theoretically, legacy, vocation, envy, pittance, compelling.

4.5 Matching ideas with the text (p.83)

Set A
a) 27, b) 14-18, c) 33-35
Set B
a) 44-45, b) 41-44, c) 28-31

The World of Nature

1.2 Matching ideas with text (p.87)

Set A   **Set B**
a = 4, b = 2   c = 3, d = 1.

1.3 Finding comparisons (p.87)

dancing (6), tossing their heads (12), they were gleeful or joyful (14), they were jocund or merry (16).
The daffodils are also compared to the many stars in the Milky Way (8).

1.4 Comparing prose with poetry (p.88)

Set A
Wordsworth uses the idea of the daffodils dancing and laughing.
They both use the word "tossed" or "tossing" and "dance" or "danced".
Wordsworth uses the word "gay" about himself and Dorothy uses it about the daffodils. Wordsworth uses the word "glance" about what he did. Dorothy says the daffodils are "ever glancing".

Set B
Wordsworth did not mention that at first they saw a few daffodils only, before coming upon the large number. He does not use the word "beautiful", nor the idea that some of them are tired and are resting their heads on stones.

1.5 Making a more detailed comparison (p.89)

Set A
Weather: threatening misty morning, the wind was furious, wind seized our breath, the lake was rough.

Set B
Flowers and plants: furze bush, hawthornes, birches, woodsorrel, anemone, violets, strawberries, pile wort, daffodils.

Main differences: Wordsworth is alone in the poem, not with his sister. There is more weather and natural detail in the diary. In the poem, Wordsworth adds the very important final idea about thinking back to the daffodil experience and getting pleasure from it.

2.1 Comparing a poem from the West with one from the East (p.89)

The difference is between picking the flower in order to observe it, thus interfering with or disturbing nature, and simply observing the flower.

3.1 Listening for general meaning (p. 92)

The picture doesn't match the text. Jude in the text is not scaring the birds.

3.2 Looking at vocabulary (p.93)

Order of explanations: appetite, alighted, thwarted desires, resemble, puny, thread of fellow feeling, tickle your breeches, simultaneously.

3.6 Reading for general meaning (p.95)

Illustration 8 matches Text K and illustration 6 matches Text L.

4.6 Deciding on the mood of a text (p.100)

amazement, sadness. The mood changes at line 31 with the idea of waging war against the snow – a sudden sense of violence and destruction.

4.8 Discussion (p.100)

Sounds are sometimes linked with meaning. "Snow" (1) itself suggests the softness of the fall and is supported by "asleep". Otherwise, as in the examples given below, rhythm can be emphasised by the repetition of sound. The "–ing" verbs suggest the immediacy of the experience (compare the use of the present form in Text C, page 5).
Other repeated sounds: tongues with tasting (21), country company (27), war is waged (31), tread toward toil (33), sorrow slumber (36).
Mood words: amazement, sorrow.

4.9 Explaining ideas (p.101)

The men have broken the magic by walking out in the snow and destroying its perfect whiteness (refer to illustration on p.98).

4.10 Looking at contrasting adjectives (p.101)

Country: still, silent, smooth, taste of peppermint, undisturbed
Town: muddy, slushy, beaten, dead
"Dead", being isolated on the last line, and being only one syllable after several two-syllable adjectives, is probably the most powerful. In its finality and bluntness it provides a complete stop to the poem.

4.11 Comparing poems (p.101)

Set A
Similarities: Snow falling in town being spoiled by people. Both poems split into two halves, the picture of the untouched snow followed by the breaking of the charm.

Set B
Differences: The country is not mentioned in Text M. The activity of the children and the workers is clearly pictured in Text M. Text N is much shorter, with shorter lines, and has no rhyme scheme.

4.12 Matching ideas with poems (p.102)

Texts O and Q contain colour contrasts, white and black, Text P looks forward to the spring and Text R expresses great enjoyment of the snow. In text M, there is the colour contrast "white" (2, 23) and "brown" (33) and the children greatly enjoy the snow, almost burying themselves (22). In Text N, "peppermint" and "muddy" suggest a colour contrast.

4.13 Discussion (p.102)

The text in the "Golden Gates" section which is about a problem caused by nature is "Plumbers" (Text D). Cold weather and snow cause people's water pipes to freeze up.

5.2 Finding specific information (p.103)

Set A
Illustration 12. The type of house, being much bigger than the native huts, shows the importance of the priest in the village.

Set B
drought. People have contracted, wrinkled stomachs, the crops had sickened or wilted and some had dried up. Cows and goats were thin.

5.5 Looking at descriptive language (p.106)

The weather: darkening clouds (24), menacing thunderstorms (26), lightning (27), slanting raindrops (30).

5.7 Deciding on a title (p.108)

An African Thunderstorm.

5.8 Comparing the language of two texts (p.108)

Set A
There are many "-ing" verb forms in both poems.
Verbs of movement: hurrying (twice), turning, whirling (twice), tossing, chasing, gather, bend, flying.

Set B
Many lines rhyme in the Bridges poem, but it is a complicated scheme beginning ABAB CBCD CDED EFEF. There is no real scheme in the Rubadiri poem, but a number of "-ing" verbs rhyme, also "out" and "about".
Sounds: whistles (14), screams (17), din of wind (19), rumble (30), crack (32), rumbling (34).

5.9 Looking at comparisons (p.108)

The wind is compared to a madman chasing nothing. The clouds are compared to a plague of locusts, pregnant females and also to dark sinister wings. The clothes are compared to tattered flags.